REA's Test Prep Books Are The Best!

(a sample of the <u>hundreds of letters</u> REA receives each year)

" I studied this guide exclusively and passed the [CLEP Introductory Sociology] test with 12 points to spare. "

Student, Dallas, TX

" This book was right on target with what was on the [CLEP Introductory Sociology] test. I highly advise studying it before you take the exam. "

Student, Washington, DC

" Your book was such a better value and was so much more complete than anything your competition has produced — and I have them all! "

Teacher, Virginia Beach, VA

" Compared to the other books that my fellow students had, your book was the most useful in helping me get a great score. "

Student, North Hollywood, CA

" Your book was responsible for my success on the exam, which helped me get into the college of my choice... I will look for REA the next time I need help. "

Student, Chesterfield, MO

" Just a short note to say thanks for the great support your book gave me in helping me pass the test... I'm on my way to a B.S. degree because of you! "

Student, Orlando, FL

(more on next page)

" I just wanted to thank you for helping me get a great score
on the AP U.S. History exam... Thank you for making great test preps! "
Student, Los Angeles, CA

" Your *Fundamentals of Engineering Exam* book was the absolute best
preparation I could have had for the exam, and it is one of the major
reasons I did so well and passed the FE on my first try. "
Student, Sweetwater, TN

" I used your book to prepare for the test and found that the advice and the
sample tests were highly relevant... Without using any other material, I earned
very high scores and will be going to the graduate school of my choice. "
Student, New Orleans, LA

" What I found in your book was a wealth of information sufficient to shore up
my basic skills in math and verbal... The section on analytical ability was
excellent. The practice tests were challenging and the answer explanations most
helpful. It certainly is the *Best Test Prep for the GRE!* "
Student, Pullman, WA

" I really appreciate the help from your excellent book. Please keep up
the great work. "
Student, Albuquerque, NM

" I am writing to thank you for your test preparation... your book helped me
immeasurably and I have nothing but praise for your *GRE* preparation."
Student, Benton Harbor, MI

THE BEST TEST PREPARATION FOR THE

CLEP
Introductory
Psychology

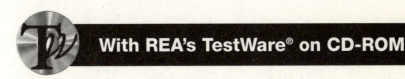

With REA's TestWare® on CD-ROM

Don J. Sharpsteen, Ph.D.
Associate Professor of Psychology
University of Missouri - Rolla
Rolla, Missouri

Research & Education Association
Visit our website at
www.rea.com

Research & Education Association
61 Ethel Road West
Piscataway, New Jersey 08854
E-mail: info@rea.com

The Best Test Preparation for the
CLEP INTRODUCTORY PSYCHOLOGY EXAM
With TestWare® on CD-ROM

Published 2011

Copyright © 2005 by Research & Education Association, Inc.
All rights reserved. No part of this book may be reproduced
in any form without permission of the publisher.

Printed in the United States of America

Library of Congress Control Number 2005901556

ISBN-13: 978-0-7386-0087-1
ISBN-10: 0-7386-0087-3

Windows® is a registered trademark of Microsoft Corporation.

About the Author

Don J. Sharpsteen was the recipient of the University of Missouri–Rolla College of Arts and Sciences Excellence in Teaching Award in 2003. He received his doctorate in Social Psychology from the University of Denver in 1988. Dr. Sharpsteen has taught courses in social psychology, personality, motivation and emotion, developmental psychology, learning, psychoanalysis, evolutionary psychology, close relationships, research methods, and statistics. His current research focuses on the cognitive representation of emotion knowledge and on the social psychological processes involved in gossip. His research has been published in a variety of psychology journals and edited books. He is currently an Associate Professor of Psychology at the University of Missouri–Rolla.

About Research & Education Association

Founded in 1959, Research & Education Association (REA) is dedicated to publishing the finest and most effective educational materials—including software, study guides, and test preps—for students in middle school, high school, college, graduate school, and beyond.

REA's Test Preparation series includes books and software for all academic levels in almost all disciplines. Research & Education Association publishes test preps for students who have not yet completed high school, as well as high school students preparing to enter college.

Today, REA's wide-ranging catalog is a leading resource for teachers, students, and professionals. We invite you to visit us at www.rea.com to find out how "REA is making the world smarter."

Acknowledgments

In addition to our author, Dr. Don Sharpsteen, we would like to thank Larry B. Kling, Vice President, Editorial, for his overall direction; John Paul Cording, Vice President, Technology, for coordinating the design, development, and testing of the software; Pam Weston, Vice President, Publishing, for setting the quality standards for production integrity and managing the publication to completion; Diane Goldschmidt, Associate Editor, for post-production quality assurance; Project Managers Reena Shah, Dipen Patel, and Amy Jamison for their tireless testing efforts; Dr. Scott Miller for technically editing the manuscript; Christine Saul, Senior Graphic Designer, for cover design; and Wende Solano for typesetting the manuscript.

CONTENTS

INSTALLING REA's TEST*ware*®

SYSTEM REQUIREMENTS

Pentium 75 MHz (300 MHz recommended), or a higher or compatible processor; Microsoft Windows 98 or later; 64 MB Available RAM; Internet Explorer 5.5 or higher.

INSTALLATION

1. Insert the CLEP Introductory Psychology TEST*ware*® CD-ROM into the CD-ROM drive.
2. If the installation doesn't begin automatically, from the Start Menu, choose the RUN command. When the RUN dialog box appears, type d:\setup (where D is the letter of your CD-ROM drive) at the prompt and click OK.
3. The installation process will begin. A dialog box proposing the directory "Program Files\REA\CLEP_IntroPsychology" will appear. If the name and location are suitable, click OK. If you wish to specify a different name or location, type it in and click OK.
4. Start the CLEP Introductory Psychology TEST*ware*® application by double-clicking on the icon.

REA's CLEP Introductory Psychology TEST*ware*® is **EASY** to **LEARN AND USE**. To achieve maximum benefits, we recommend that you take a few minutes to go through the on-screen tutorial on your computer.

SSD ACCOMMODATIONS FOR STUDENTS WITH DISABILITIES

Many students qualify for extra time to take the CLEP Introductory Psychology exam, and our TEST*ware*® can be adapted to accommodate your time extension. This allows you to practice under the same extended-time accommodations that you will receive on the actual test day. To customize your TEST*ware*® to suit the most common extensions, visit our website at *www.rea.com/ssd*.

TECHNICAL SUPPORT

REA's TEST*ware*® is backed by customer and technical support. For questions about **installation or operation of your software**, contact us at:

Research & Education Association
Phone: (732) 819-8880 (9 a.m. to 5 p.m. ET, Monday–Friday)
Fax: (732) 819-8808
Website: http://www.rea.com
E-mail: info@rea.com

Note to Windows XP Users: In order for the TEST*ware*® to function properly, please install and run the application under the same computer-administrator level user account. Installing the TEST*ware*® as one user and running it as another could cause file access path conflicts.

CLEP INTRODUCTORY PSYCHOLOGY
Independent Study Schedule

The following study schedule allows for thorough preparation for the CLEP Introductory Psychology Exam. Although it is designed for four weeks, it can be reduced to a two-week course by collapsing the first two-week periods into one. Be sure to set aside enough time—at least two hours each day—to study. But no matter which study schedule works best for you, the more time you spend studying, the more prepared and relaxed you will feel on the day of the exam.

Week	Activity
1	Read and study Chapter 1, which will introduce you to the CLEP Introductory Psychology Exam. Then take Practice Test 1 on CD-ROM to determine your strengths and weaknesses. Review your explanations, paying particular attention to the questions you answered incorrectly. You can then determine the areas in which you need to strengthen your skills.
2 & 3	Carefully read and study the Psychology Review included in this book.
4	Take Practice Test 2 on CD-ROM to determine your strengths and weaknesses. Review your explanations, paying particular attention to the questions you answered incorrectly. If there are any types of questions or particular subjects that seem difficult to you, review those subjects by studying again the appropriate sections of the Psychology Review.

Note: If you care to, and time allows, retake Practice Tests 1 and 2. This will help strengthen the areas in which your performance may still be lagging and build your overall confidence.

CHAPTER 1

Passing the CLEP Introductory Psychology Exam

Chapter 1

PASSING THE CLEP INTRODUCTORY PSYCHOLOGY EXAM

ABOUT THIS BOOK & TEST*ware*®

This book provides you with complete preparation for the CLEP Introductory Psychology Computer-Based Test, or CBT. Inside you will find a concise review of the subject matter, as well as tips and strategies for test-taking. We also give you two practice tests, which are based on the official CLEP Introductory Psychology Exam. Our practice tests contain every type of question that you can expect to encounter on the actual exam. Following each practice test you will find an answer key with detailed explanations designed to help you more completely understand the test material.

The practice exams in this book and software package are included in two formats: in printed format in this book, and in TEST*ware*® format on the enclosed CD. **We strongly recommend that you begin your preparation with the TEST*ware*® practice exams.** The software provides the added benefits of automatic scoring and enforced time conditions.

ABOUT THE EXAM

Who takes the CLEP Introductory Psychology Exam and what is it used for?

CLEP (College-Level Examination Program) examinations are typically taken by people who have acquired knowledge outside the classroom and wish to bypass certain college courses and earn college credit. The CLEP is designed to reward students for learning—no matter where or how that knowledge was acquired. The CLEP is the most widely accepted credit-by-examination program in the United States, with more than 2,900 colleges and universities granting credit for satisfactory scores on CLEP exams.

Although most CLEP examinees are adults returning to college, many graduating high school seniors, enrolled college students, and international students also take the exams to earn college credit or to demonstrate their ability to perform at the college level. There are no prerequisites, such as age or educational status, for taking CLEP examinations. However, because policies on granting credits vary among colleges, you should contact the particular institution from which you wish to receive CLEP credit.

There are two categories of CLEP examinations:

1. CLEP General Examinations, which are five separate tests that cover material usually taken as requirements during the first two years of college. CLEP General Examinations are available for English Composition (with or without essay), Humanities, Mathematics, Natural Sciences, and Social Sciences and History.

2. CLEP Subject Examinations, like the CLEP Introductory Psychology Exam, which include material usually covered in an undergraduate course with a similar title.

Who administers the exam?

The CLEP Exams are developed by the College Board, administered by Educational Testing Service (ETS), and involve the assistance of educators throughout the United States. The test development process is designed and implemented to ensure that the content and difficulty level of the test are appropriate.

When and where is the exam given?

The CLEP Introductory Psychology Exam is administered each month throughout the year at more than 1,400 test centers in the United States and can be arranged for candidates abroad on request. To find the test center nearest you and to register for the exam, you should obtain a copy of the free booklet *Information for Candidates and Registration Form.* It is available at most colleges where CLEP credit is granted, or by contacting:

CLEP Services
P.O. Box 6600
Princeton, NJ 08541-6600
Phone: (800) 257-9558
Fax: (609) 771-7088
Website: http://www.collegeboard.com

Military personnel and CLEP

CLEP exams are available free of charge to eligible military personnel and eligible civilian employees. The College Board has developed a paper-based version of 14 high-volume/high-pass-rate CLEP tests for DANTES Test Centers. Contact the Educational Services Officer or Navy College Education Specialist for more information. Also, visit the College Board website for details about CLEP opportunities for military personnel.

Eligible U.S. veterans can claim reimbursement for CLEP exams and administration fees pursuant to provisions of the Veterans' Benefits Improvement Act of 2004. For details on eligibility and submitting a claim for reimbursement, visit the U.S. Department of Veterans Affairs website at *www.gibill.va.gov/pamphlets/testing.htm*.

SSD Accommodations for Students with Disabilities

Many students qualify for extra time to take the CLEP Introductory Psychology Exam, but you must make these arrangements in advance with the test administrator at the college where you plan to take the exam. For information, contact:

College Board Services for Students with Disabilities
PO Box 6226
Princeton, NJ 08541-6226
Phone: (609) 771-7137 Monday through Friday,
        8 a.m. to 6 p.m. (Eastern time)
TTY: (609) 882-4118
Fax: (609) 771-7944
E-mail: ssd@info.collegeboard.org

Our TEST*ware*® can be adapted to accommodate your time extension. This allows you to practice under the same extended-time accommodations that you will receive on the actual test day. To customize your TEST*ware*® to suit the most common extensions, visit our website at *www.rea.com/ssd*.

HOW TO USE THIS BOOK

What do I study first?

Read over the course review and the suggestions for test-taking, take the first practice test to determine your area(s) of weakness, and then go back and focus your study on those specific problems. Studying the reviews thoroughly will reinforce the basic skills you will need to do well on the exam. Make sure to take the practice tests to become familiar with the format and procedures involved with taking the actual exam.

To best utilize your study time, follow our Independent Study Schedule, which you'll find in the front of this book. The schedule is based on a six-week program, but can be condensed to three weeks if necessary by collapsing each two-week period into one.

When should I start studying?

It is never too early to start studying for the CLEP Introductory Psychology. The earlier you begin, the more time you will have to sharpen your skills. Do not procrastinate! Cramming is *not* an effective way to study, since it does not allow you the time needed to learn the test material. The sooner you learn the format of the exam, the more time you will have to familiarize yourself with it.

FORMAT AND CONTENT OF THE CLEP EXAM

The CLEP Introductory Psychology covers the material one would find in a college-level introductory Psychology class. The exam stresses basic facts and principles, as well as general theoretical approaches used by psychologists.

The approximate breakdown of topics is as follows:

8–9%	History, Approaches, Methods
8–9%	Biological Bases of Behavior
7–8%	Sensation and Perception
5–6%	States of Consciousness
10–11%	Learning
8–9%	Cognition
7–8%	Motivation and Emotion
8–9%	Developmental Psychology
7–8%	Personality
8–9%	Psychological Disorders and Health
7–8%	Treatment of Psychological Disorders
7–8%	Social Psychology
3–4%	Statistics, Tests, and Measurement

The actual CLEP Introductory Psychology Exam contains 95 multiple-choice questions. The practice tests in this book and on the accompanying CD contain 100 multiple-choice questions. This will allow you extra practice in content knowledge and time management.

PRACTICE-TEST RAW SCORE CONVERSION TABLE *

Raw Score	Scaled Score	Course Grade	Raw Score	Scaled Score	Course Grade
100	80	A	48	49	C
99	80	A	47	49	C
98	80	A	46	48	C
97	79	A	45	48	C
96	79	A	44	47	C
95	78	A	43	47	C
94	78	A	42	47	C
93	77	A	41	47	C
92	77	A	40	46	D
91	76	A	39	46	D
90	75	A	38	45	D
89	74	A	37	45	D
88	73	A	36	44	D
87	73	A	35	44	D
86	72	A	34	43	D
85	72	A	33	43	D
84	71	A	32	42	D
83	70	A	31	41	D
82	70	A	30	40	F
81	69	A	29	39	F
80	69	A	28	38	F
79	68	A	27	37	F
78	67	A	26	36	F
77	66	A	25	35	F
76	66	A	24	34	F
75	65	A	23	34	F
74	64	A	22	33	F
73	63	A	21	33	F
72	63	A	20	32	F
71	62	A	19	32	F
70	61	A	18	31	F
69	61	A	17	31	F
68	60	A	16	30	F
67	59	A	15	29	F
66	59	A	14	28	F
65	58	B	13	28	F
64	57	B	12	27	F
63	57	B	11	27	F
62	56	B	10	26	F
61	56	B	9	25	F
60	55	B	8	24	F
59	55	B	7	23	F
58	54	B	6	22	F
57	54	B	5	21	F
56	53	B	4	20	F
55	53	B	3	20	F
54	52	B	2	20	F
53	52	B	1	20	F
52	51	C	0	20	F
51	51	C			
50	50	C			
49	50	C			

*This table is provided for scoring REA practice tests only. With the advent of computer-based testing, the College-Level Examination Program uses a single across-the-board credit-granting score of 50 for all CLEP computer-based exams. Nonetheless, on account of the different skills being measured and the unique content requirements of each test, the actual number of correct answers needed to reach 50 will vary. A 50 is calibrated to equate with performance that would warrant the grade C in the corresponding introductory college course.

ABOUT OUR COURSE REVIEW

The review in this book provides you with a complete background of all the pertinent theorists, principles, and concepts of Psychology. It will help reinforce the facts you have already learned while better shaping your understanding of the discipline as a whole. By using the review in conjunction with the practice tests, you should be well prepared to take the CLEP Introductory Psychology.

SCORING THE BOOK'S PRACTICE TESTS

How do I score my practice tests?

The CLEP Introductory Psychology is scored on a scale of 20 to 80. To score your practice tests, count up the number of correct answers. This is your total raw score. Convert your raw score to a scaled score using the conversion table on the previous page. (**Note:** The conversion table provides only an estimate of your scaled score. Scaled scores can and do vary over time, and in no case should a sample test be taken as a precise predictor of test performance. Nonetheless, our scoring table allows you to judge your level of performance within a reasonable scoring range.)

When will I receive my score report?

The test administrator will print out a full Candidate Score Report for you immediately upon your completion of the exam. Your scores are reported only to you, unless you ask to have them sent elsewhere. If you want your scores reported to a college or other institution, you must indicate this in the test software when you take the examination. Since your scores are kept on file for 20 years, you can also request transcripts from Educational Testing Service at a later date.

STUDYING FOR THE CLEP EXAM

It is very important for you to choose the time and place for studying that works best for you. Some students may set aside a certain number of hours every morning, while others may choose to study at night before going to sleep. Other students may study during the day, while waiting on a line, or even while eating lunch. Only you can determine when and where your study time will be most effective. But be consistent and use your time wisely. Work out a study routine and stick to it!

When you take the practice tests, try to make your testing conditions as much like the actual test as possible. Turn your television and radio off, and sit down at a quiet table free from distraction. Make sure to time yourself. Start off by setting a timer for the time that is allotted for each section, and be sure to reset the timer for the appropriate amount of time when you start a new section.

As you complete each practice test, score your test and thoroughly review the explanations to the questions you answered incorrectly; however, do not review too much at one time. Concentrate on one problem area at a time by reviewing the question and explanation, and by studying our review until you are confident that you completely understand the material.

Keep track of your scores. By doing so, you will be able to gauge your progress and discover general weaknesses in particular sections. You should carefully study the reviews that cover your areas of difficulty, as this will build your skills in those areas.

TEST-TAKING TIPS

Although you may not be familiar with computer-based standardized tests such as the CLEP Introductory Psychology, there are many ways to acquaint yourself with this type of examination and to help alleviate your test-taking anxieties. Listed below are ways to help you become accustomed to the CLEP, some of which may be applied to other standardized tests as well.

Know the format of the CBT. CLEP CBTs are not adaptive but rather fixed-length tests. In a sense, this makes them kin to the familiar paper-and-pencil exam in that you have the same flexibility to go back and review your work in each section. Moreover, the format hasn't changed a great deal from the paper-and-pencil CLEP.

Read all of the possible answers. Just because you think you have found the correct response, do not automatically assume that it is the best answer. Read through each choice to be sure that you are not making a mistake by jumping to conclusions.

Use the process of elimination. Go through each answer to a question and eliminate as many of the answer choices as possible. By eliminating just two answer choices, you give yourself a better chance of getting the item correct, since there will only be three choices left from which to make your guess. Remember, your score is based only on the number of questions you answer *correctly*.

Work quickly and steadily. You will have only 90 minutes to work on 95 questions, so work quickly and steadily to avoid focusing on any one question too long. Taking the practice tests in this book will help you learn to budget your time.

Acquaint yourself with the CBT screen. Familiarize yourself with the CLEP CBT screen beforehand by logging on to the College Board website. Waiting until test day to see what it looks like in the pretest tutorial risks experiencing needless anxiety into your testing experience. Also, familiarizing yourself with the directions and format of the exam will save you valuable time on the day of the actual test.

Be sure that your answer registers before you go to the next item. Look at the screen to see that your mouse-click causes the pointer to darken the proper oval. This takes less effort than darkening an oval on paper, but don't lull yourself into taking less care!

THE DAY OF THE EXAM

Preparing for the CLEP Exam

On the day of the test, you should wake up early (hopefully after a decent night's rest) and have a good breakfast. Make sure to dress comfortably, so that you are not distracted by being too hot or too cold while taking the test. Also plan to arrive at the test center early. This will allow you to collect your thoughts and relax before the test, and will also spare you the anxiety that comes with being late. As an added incentive to make sure you arrive early, keep in mind that no one will be allowed into the test session after the test has begun.

Before you leave for the test center, make sure that you have your Registration-Administration form, Social Security number, a government-issued photo ID with your signature (i.e., driver's license, passport, state-issued ID, or current alien registration card), a second ID with photo and/or signature, and the fee. You will not be admitted to the test center if you do not have proper identification.

If you would like, you may wear a watch to the test center. However, you may not wear one that makes noise, because it may disturb the other test-takers. No cell phones, PDAs, scrap paper, dictionaries, textbooks, notebooks, briefcases, or packages will be permitted, and drinking, smoking, and eating are prohibited.

Good luck on the CLEP Introductory Psychology Exam!

▼

CHAPTER 2

History and Methods

Chapter 2

HISTORY AND METHODS

PSYCHOLOGY'S HISTORY

Psychology—the scientific study of human behavior and mental processes—began as an attempt to answer philosophical questions about human nature using the methods borrowed from physics, physiology, and other sciences. **Wilhelm Wundt,** who was educated in physiology, set up the first psychology laboratory in Leipzig, Germany, in order to scientifically study how people sense and perceive the world around them. But debate soon arose over what, specifically, the domain of psychology should be and how it should be studied.

Structuralists believed that consciousness was made up of basic elements that were combined in different ways to produce different perceptions, much like hydrogen and oxygen would form water if combined in the right way. Thus, structuralists wanted to discover the form, or basic elements, of mental experience.

The technique favored by structuralists for examining mental experience was **introspection**. Introspection involves reporting on one's own conscious thoughts and feelings. Although Wundt and other structuralists (such as **Edward Titchener**, who set up the first psychology lab in the U.S.) emphasized accurate measurement and replicability in their studies, introspection was nevertheless a subjective way to study consciousness, and couldn't be used to study children and animals. It eventually fell into disfavor.

Functionalists, on the other hand, were less interested in what made up mental experiences than in how mental experiences or processes were adaptive, or functional, for people. Functionalists (perhaps the most famous being **William James**) believed that consciousness, and behavior in general, helped people and animals adjust to their environments. Understanding the mind meant understanding what the mind accomplished.

Currently, psychologists study both the structure and functions of behavior. Those who study infant-caregiver attachment behavior, for example, might examine the structure of attachment (such as the feelings and behaviors that arise in response to separations), as well as the functions of attachment (how those feelings and behaviors keep the infant close to the caregiver). But, as described in the next section, what any given psychologist has to say about those structures and functions will depend on his or her theoretical orientation.

MODERN APPROACHES TO UNDERSTANDING HUMAN BEHAVIOR

Because of its roots in philosophy, psychology has to deal with many questions that probably can't be answered empirically: Do people have free will, or is their behavior determined only by past experiences? Are people basically good, or inherently selfish? Can explanations of behavior be reduced to physiological activity, or is it necessary to consider complex interactions among many factors? Over the last century, at least five philosophical orientations have come to dominate answers to those sorts of questions and to guide psychological research and theory.

Those who adopt a **biological approach** to studying behavior focus on understanding how physiological and biochemical processes might produce psychological phenomena. From this perspective, explanations for behavior are ultimately reducible to the workings of genes, the nervous system, hormones, neurotransmitters, and so forth.

According to those who favor a **psychodynamic approach,** thoughts, feelings, and behaviors stem from the interaction of innate drives and society's restrictions on the expression of those drives. For **Sigmund Freud**, the most important urges are the sexual and aggressive ones. Society doesn't generally approve of unrestricted sex and aggression, so we all face conflicts between getting our needs met and alienating other people. How we resolve those conflicts, primarily during the first few years of life, determines our personality. Later psychodynamic theorists focused on attachment and interpersonal connection as a primary drive. The reasons for much of your behavior, then, are unconscious, and rooted in childhood.

Those who take a **behaviorist approach** explain behavior primarily in terms of learned responses to predictable patterns of environmental stimuli. Pavlov's studies of classical conditioning and Skinner's studies of operant conditioning exemplify this approach. More than with other approaches, those who are behaviorists often study animals in order to glean general principles of learning that might then be applied to humans.

The **cognitive approach** developed in large part as a reaction against behaviorism. Behaviorists preferred to avoid explanations of behavior that didn't involve observable events (i.e., stimuli), which meant that references to "expectations," "feelings," "thoughts," and so on were frowned upon. The cognitive approach focuses on explaining behavior in terms of precisely those sorts of things. Thus, cognitivists might study problem solving, attention, expectations, memory, and other thought processes.

The central claim of the **humanistic approach** is that people aren't merely machines whose behaviors are determined for them by a genetic code, a conflicted childhood, brushes with stimuli, or cold mental calculations. Instead, humanists see people as motivated by a desire for optimal growth and development (i.e., **self-actualization**). From their perspective, each one of us comes with his or her own unique set of desires, abilities, skills, and needs, and, in order to be happy and well-adjusted, must be able to express those desires, abilities, and so forth. Because they see people as basically good, they tend to focus on positive aspects of development (how to feel good about yourself, for example).

RESEARCH METHODS

Because psychology is a science, information about human behavior is collected in systematic, objective, and replicable ways—primarily through experimentation and correlational studies.

In **experiments**, researchers assess cause-and-effect relationships between at least two variables. The "cause" is represented by the **independent variable** and will always involve treating subjects in at least two different ways: Subjects in the **experimental group** are exposed to whatever the presumed "cause" is; those in the **control group** are not exposed to the "cause." The "effect" is represented by the **dependent variable** and will typically involve measuring how subjects behave. Because subjects are assigned **randomly** to each experimental condition (in order to ensure that the average behavior of the two groups would be the same prior to the manipulation), and because there is only one difference in how the experimental and control groups are treated, any difference in the behavior of those two groups must be due to that treatment (i.e., the independent variable).

It's possible that subjects in an experimental group could behave differently than they normally would only because they know they're being exposed to a special treatment. This is called the **placebo effect**. In order to determine the extent to which this might be happening, control-group subjects are sometimes told that they, too, are receiving a special treatment even when they're not. This fake special treatment (the classic example of which occurs when a pill contains inert substances rather than the drug received by the experimental group) is called a **placebo**. If subjects don't know whether they're receiving the drug or the placebo, the experiment is called a **blind study**. It's possible that experimenters can unwittingly influence results by knowing which subjects received which treatment. Therefore, they also may not know whether they're delivering the placebo or the drug. This type of experiment is called a **double-blind study**.

Correlational studies also involve assessing the relationship between two variables, but because neither variable is manipulated, there is no way to determine whether changes in one variable cause changes in the other; only how changes in one are related to changes in the other can be determined. There are two ways in which these variables might be related. A **positive relationship** means that high scores on one variable tend to be paired with high scores on the other variable (and low scores with low scores); for example, height and weight have a positive correlation – generally speaking, as one increases so does the other. A **negative relationship** means that high scores on one variable tend to be paired with low scores on the other variable. Job satisfaction and absenteeism are negatively correlated; as job satisfaction increases, absentee rates decline. In addition to the direction of the relationship, a **correlation coefficient** will describe the strength of the relationship: The coefficient ranges from -1.0 to 1.0, with higher absolute values representing stronger relationships. Notice, then, that a correlation of, say, -.73 is just as strong as a correlation of +.73; they differ only in the direction of the relationship. A low correlation indicates that there is not a consistent relationship between two variables. For example, height and IQ have a low correlation.

In **surveys**, participants are asked to fill out questionnaires that ask them about their opinions, attitudes, or behaviors. Researchers can determine the frequency with which people endorse or do various things, and can also determine relationships among those behaviors and attitudes.

Case studies involve in-depth analysis of only one person. Freud's theory of psychoanalysis was built upon a series of case studies.

Behavior might also be studied as it occurs in real-life settings. This is called **naturalistic observation**. Two things to be aware of when performing a naturalistic study include being unobtrusive (i.e., not interfering with ongoing behavior) and having high agreement among observers as to what is happening. Agreement among observers is a measure of "**inter-judge**," "**inter-rater**," or "**inter-observer**" reliability.

CHAPTER 3

Biological Bases
of Behavior

Chapter 3

BIOLOGICAL BASES OF BEHAVIOR

Nothing psychological can happen without a body and communication among its parts (the brain, muscles, glands, organs, nerves, arms, legs, and so forth). The field of **behavioral neuroscience** is concerned with how this communication happens and how behavior is influenced by it. In large part it deals with the **nervous system**—an organization of neurons, neurotransmitters, and brain structures that serves as the framework for moving information throughout the body.

NEURONS

Thinking, feeling, or doing things requires that information about the environment or the body is transferred from one place inside you to another. There are some parts of the body (i.e., **sense receptors**) that detect heat, or light, or touch and then pass information about those stimuli on to the brain, thereby triggering thoughts about those things and/or causing behavioral responses to occur. The pathways for this communication are called **neurons** (i.e., nerve cells), and there are three different types. **Sensory neurons** (or **afferent neurons**) take in information from body tissues and sense organs, and transmit it to the spinal cord and brain; **motor neurons** (or **efferent neurons**) send information in the opposite direction; and **interneurons** (or **association neurons**) are neurons that communicate with other neurons.

As shown in Figure 3.1, neurons consist of a **cell body** (which contains structures that help to keep the cell alive and functioning), **dendrites** (short, bushy fibers that take information in from outside the cell), **axons** (relatively long fibers—some extending up to several feet—that pass information along to other nerve cells, to glands, or to muscles), and, on some neurons, a **myelin sheath** (a fatty tissue that surrounds the axon and accelerates transmission of information).

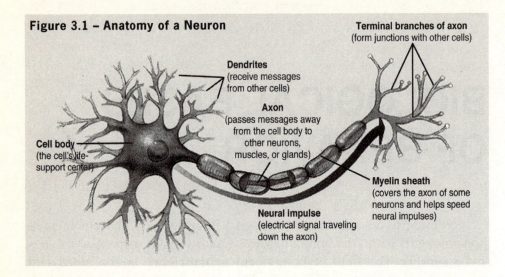

Figure 3.1 – Anatomy of a Neuron

Terminal branches of axon
(form junctions with other cells)

Dendrites
(receive messages from other cells)

Axon
(passes messages away from the cell body to other neurons, muscles, or glands)

Cell body
(the cell's life-support center)

Myelin sheath
(covers the axon of some neurons and helps speed neural impulses)

Neural impulse
(electrical signal traveling down the axon)

Neurons do their work through the use of electrical impulses and neurotransmitters. In the first case, a signal (i.e., information) from a sense receptor or another neuron, coming in through a neuron's dendrites, gets passed along when it triggers an **action potential**, or electrical impulse, that travels down the axon and then triggers activity in whichever neurons, muscles, or glands join up with that axon.

That action potential is chemically generated: The fluid inside a "resting" axon contains predominantly negatively charged **ions** (electrically charged atoms), whereas the fluid outside the axon contains more positively charged sodium ions. This arrangement, called the **resting potential,** is maintained because the axon's membrane won't let positive ions into the cell unless the cell receives a signal from the dendrites. When that signal arrives, the part of the axon nearest the dendrites is "depolarized" by that signal, allowing positive ions in. That then depolarizes the next part of the axon and the action potential continues in that way down the axon (like dominoes falling) to its destination. During a **refractory period**, the neuron pumps out the sodium ions and can then fire again.

NEUROTRANSMITTERS

The parts of a single neuron are physically connected, so electrical signals are able to travel from one end of the neuron to the other without interruption. Between neurons, however, is a small gap. The junction where the end of one neuron meets the beginning of another is called a **synapse** and the gap between them—less than one millionth of an inch—is called the **synaptic gap**. Communication across this gap is accomplished with neurotransmitters, rather than with electrical impulses.

Neurotransmitters are chemical molecules contained in **vesicles**, or sacs, within the **axon terminal** (i.e., the knoblike end of the axon). When an action potential arrives at the terminal, the neurotransmitters are released into the synaptic cleft. They then bind to receptor sites on the next neuron's dendrites. Depending on a variety of factors (e.g., the presence of other chemicals or input from other neurons), this process makes the receiving neuron either more or less likely to fire. Any excess neurotransmitter left in the gap either breaks down through a process called enzymatic degradation or is absorbed back into a neuron through a process called reuptake.

Different neurotransmitters affect different neurons. Because different neural pathways are made up of different neurons and have different functions, each neurotransmitter affects behavior differently. **Serotonin**, for example, helps control arousal and sleep. Low levels of serotonin in the brain are typical of some forms of depression. Drugs that mimic a particular neurotransmitter or make more of it available by blocking its reuptake are called **agonists**. Some anti-depressants (e.g., Prozac) increase the level of available serotonin by inhibiting uptake. Drugs that block a neurotransmitter's receptor sites or inhibit its release are called **antagonists**.

SUB-SYSTEMS OF THE NERVOUS SYSTEM

Figure 3.2 shows the divisions of the nervous system. The **central nervous system** includes the brain, which of course controls many physiological and psychological functions, and the spinal cord, which enables reflexive behavior and relays information to the brain from elsewhere in the body.

Figure 3.2: The divisions of the nervous system.

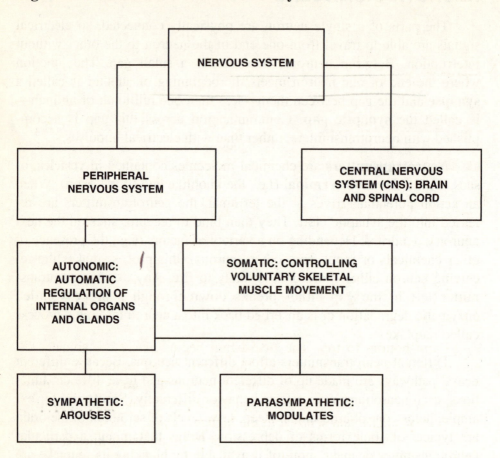

The **peripheral nervous system** (PNS) includes the sensory and motor neurons that connect the brain and spinal cord to the rest of the body. The PNS is divided into the somatic nervous system and the autonomic nervous system. The **somatic nervous system** accomplishes two functions which, together, allow you to operate in the external environment. First, it carries information from muscles, sense organs, and skin to the central nervous system (allowing the sensations of pressure, pain, and temperature, among other things). Second, it carries messages from the central nervous system to skeletal muscles, allowing for voluntary movement.

In contrast, the **autonomic nervous system** regulates the body's internal environment, controlling the functioning of glands, organs, and some muscles. Although this control can sometimes be done consciously (with the help of the central nervous system), it is generally done involuntarily (i.e., "autonomously").

The autonomic system can, in turn, be broken down into two main divisions that work together in a complementary way. The **sympathetic nervous system** prepares you for action. When you become aware of something alarming, for example, the sympathetic system quickens your heartbeat, slows your digestion, raises the level of sugar in your blood, widens your arteries, and stimulates your sweat glands. In contrast, the **parasympathetic nervous system** deactivates the systems mobilized by the sympathetic nervous system and is in operation during states of relaxation. Parasympathetic responses include decreased heart rate, breathing rate and digestive functioning.

BRAIN ORGANIZATION

Neurons in the brain work together as **neural networks**—groups of neurons that serve similar functions. Although brain organization is typically described in terms of different parts of the brain that tend to serve different functions, a network's neurons can, in fact, be spread physically throughout many areas of the brain.

From bottom to top: The **brainstem** begins where the spinal cord enters the skull and is, biologically, the brain's oldest region. It is responsible for controlling breathing and heartbeat. The **thalamus** sits on top of the brainstem and receives information about touch, taste, sight, and hearing (but not smell), and sends it to the higher brain regions. The **reticular formation** runs through both these parts of the brain and is known mostly for its control of arousal and sleep, but it also filters incoming stimuli and sends information to other parts of the brain. The most notable function of the **cerebellum**, which is at the rear base of the brainstem, is the coordination of voluntary movement.

The **limbic system** sits between these older parts of the brain and the more recently evolved cerebral cortex and comprises several component structures. The **hippocampus** processes memory. The **amygdala** influences fear and anger. In a variety of animals, damage in one area of the amygdala will produce violent rage, whereas damage in another will produce placidity. Neural networks within the **hypothalamus** influence hunger, thirst, and sexual behavior, among other things. The hypothalamus also controls the **pituitary gland**, which is a sort of "master gland," influencing the release of hormones from other glands. (**Hormones** are chemical messengers that are produced in one kind of tissue, travel through the bloodstream, and then affect the functions of some other tissue, including the brain. These hormones, and the glands that produce them, constitute the **endocrine system**.)

The **cerebral cortex**—the outer covering of the brain—is primarily involved in motor, cognitive, and sensory processes. Each of the two hemispheres (left and right) of the cerebral cortex is divided into four regions, each having a variety of functions. The **frontal lobes** (just behind the forehead) play a part in coordinating movement and in higher level thinking such as planning and predicting the consequences of behaviors. They also are involved in speech: Someone with damage to **Broca's area**, which is in the frontal lobe, can usually understand speech, but can only speak slowly and with great difficulty; someone with damage to **Wernicke's area** can physically speak, but will only string together meaningless words.

The **parietal lobes** are at the top of the head, but behind the frontal lobes. They are involved in the sense of touch, among other things, and allow us to keep tabs on where our hands and feet are and what they're up to. Just above and on either side of the ears are the **temporal lobes**, which are involved in hearing. At the base of the skull, in the back, are the **occipital lobes**. These areas are involved in vision.

CHAPTER 4

Sensation and Perception

Chapter 4

SENSATION AND PERCEPTION

Energy is all around us. **Sensation** has to do with transforming energy from the stimuli outside us (e.g., light waves or sound waves) into neural energy that can be used for **perception**, which involves mentally creating an image of the outside world.

SENSATION

Psychophysics is the area of psychology that addresses the topic of sensation; the topic includes the levels of intensity at which we can detect stimuli, how sensitive we are to changes in stimulation, and how psychological factors influence our ability to sense stimuli. According to **signal detection theory**, our ability to notice a stimulus will vary due to psychological factors including motivation, past experience, and expectations. The minimum stimulation needed for a given person to detect a given stimulus (an odor, taste, sound, etc.) is called an **absolute threshold**. It is typically thought of as the intensity necessary for a stimulus to be detected 50 percent of the time that it's presented.

We often want or need to detect differences between stimuli, as well, not just their presence or absence. Is that burglary suspect taller than the burglar you saw, or is he the same height? Do these speakers have clearer sounds than the other ones? The smallest difference a person can detect between two similar stimuli is called the **just noticeable difference** (or **jnd**) or the **difference threshold**. According to **Weber's Law**, this threshold increases in proportion to the intensity or magnitude of the stimuli. That is, any given difference is harder to notice with intense, powerful stimuli than with weaker ones. The difference in brightness between a 40-watt light bulb and a 60-watt light bulb, for example, would be easier to detect than the difference between a 70-watt bulb and a 90-watt bulb, even though the absolute difference between them (20 watts) is the same.

One reason this matters is that stimuli have to change in some way in order to remain noticeable. When exposed to an unchanging stimulus, the nerve cells involved in detecting it begin to fire less frequently and our sensitivity to the stimulus diminishes. This is called **sensory adaptation**. Sensory adaptation predisposes us (and other organisms, of course) to attend to stimuli that matter to us and not attend to stimuli that don't.

The nervous system's idea of a stimulus isn't necessarily the same as the mind's, though. Individual neurons in the visual cortex, for example, respond to highly specific aspects of visual scenes. For instance, one of these **feature detectors** might only respond to a line that is tilted at a 20-degree angle (and go quiet when the same line is tilted to a different angle). Information from this feature detection cell, and others that are triggered at the same time, is then passed on to cells that will only respond to more complex patterns, such as faces at a particular angle or a leg moving in some specific direction. Clusters of "supercells" then integrate this information and will fire if the collective cues are indicative of, say, someone approaching.

The visual system, auditory system, and so forth can represent the stimuli in our environment amazingly accurately, but what we think we sense isn't always an accurate representation of what we really are sensing. For one thing, the amount of information we can hold in our awareness is less than the amount of information available from our environment. Thus **selective attention**, as this is called, illustrates that our ideas about reality have to be chosen, organized, and interpreted, not simply detected. Constructing meaning out of sensation is what **perception** is about.

PERCEPTION

Gestalt psychologists were among the first to formulate rules by which the brain pieces together meaningful experiences out of fragments of sensation (the German word gestalt means "a whole" or "a form"). Much of their research shows that, in a variety of ways, the mind fills in gaps in our sensations. Thus, for example, we may perceive a whole circle, when in reality there are only disconnected parts of a circle falling in a circular pattern.

We're also capable of seeing objects in three dimensions (a perception), despite the fact that the images on our retinas are only in two dimensions (a sensation). **Depth perception**, as this is called, is what allows us to estimate distances between ourselves and the objects we see. We do this with the help of two types of cues.

Binocular cues require both eyes. Because of the spacing between our eyes, each retina receives a slightly different picture of the world. This **retinal disparity** is one cue to distance. Holding a finger close to the nose, the left eye sees mostly just the left side of the finger, whereas the right eye sees the right side of the finger. But if the finger is held out as far away from you as possible, the two eyes instead pick up very similar images. Low retinal disparity, then, is a crude indicator that an object is relatively far away. A second binocular cue to distance is **convergence**, the extent to which the eyes must turn inward (toward the nose) to view an object. Greater convergence indicates a closer object.

Monocular cues to depth perception require only one eye. **Linear perspective**, for example, refers to the fact that parallel lines appear to converge as they get farther away. Thus, when looking at railroad tracks, their distance (and that of the train that's on them) is perceived as greater when the two tracks appear closer together. **Motion parallax** (or **relative motion**) refers to the apparent movement of stable objects as we ourselves move. Driving down the road in a car, for example, you might be looking at a tree in the distance (this would be your **fixation point**). Objects closer than the tree would appear to be moving backward, and the nearer they are, the faster they seem to be moving; objects that are more distant than the fixation point seem to move with you, but more slowly as they get farther away. When one object partially blocks out another, we perceive it as closer. This is called **interposition**. **Texture gradients** also influence judgments of depth. Objects that are close tend to appear distinct (thus having a "coarse" texture), whereas those that are far away tend to blend together into an indistinct, fine texture.

These perceptual cues are largely "wired in" to our brains but, to some extent, our experiences shape our perceptions. This has been demonstrated in studies of **sensory restriction**. For example, if kittens are kept from seeing for several months when they're infants, they are unable later to tell the difference between objects of different shapes (a circle and a square, for instance). Without appropriate stimulation, the cells in their cortex don't develop the inter-connections that would allow this sort of perception. This doesn't happen when the sensory restriction takes place during adulthood, suggesting that there is a **critical period** during which exposure to appropriate stimuli is required in order for the various perceptual skills to develop.

Another way in which experience shapes perception is through **perceptual sets**: predispositions to perceive one thing and not another. In line with gender stereotypes, people often perceive a crying baby to be weak and scared if they believe it's a girl, but strong and mad if it's a boy. Similarly, you might perceive the sound of water hitting the spout in your tub to be the sound of a phone ringing, if you're expecting someone to call while you're in the shower.

The general principle: Processing information about the environment occurs in both a **bottom-up** fashion (from simple sensory receptors to more complex neural networks) and a **top-down** fashion (from expectations, motives, and contextual cues to raw sensory data).

CHAPTER 5

Consciousness

Chapter 5

CONSCIOUSNESS

Consciousness is the state of being aware. It's reflecting on the environment or on internal experiences rather than simply reacting to them. Much of what psychologists study is the various uses to which consciousness can be put, such as thinking, problem-solving, learning, and memory—things we do while awake and in a "normal" state of mind. But chapters on consciousness in introductory psychology textbooks typically focus on describing and explaining the cyclical nature of conscious states—repeated patterns of waking and sleeping in several distinct and predictable stages—and on "altered" states of consciousness such as dreams and hypnosis.

PATTERNS OF WAKING AND SLEEPING

In humans (and other species), hormone levels, body temperature, and wakefulness rise and fall in predictable ways during the course of a day. In other words, these characteristics have a **circadian rhythm**; their predictability stems from their being synchronized with the parts of the day ("circadian" is Latin for "about the day"). As an example, body temperature typically begins to rise in the early morning, peaks around midday, dips in mid-afternoon, and then drops in the late evening.

There is also a biological rhythm for **sleep**. During sleep, brain waves (and the quality of sleep) cycle through a series of five stages every 90 minutes or so. These stages are distinguished, in part, by the type and appearance of brain waves involved in each (**brain waves** are electrical currents in the brain as shown graphically on an **EEG**, or electroencephalogram). Examples of different types of brain waves are presented in Figure 5.1.

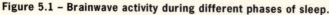

Figure 5.1 – Brainwave activity during different phases of sleep.

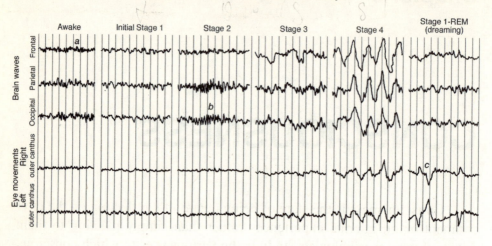

In an awake but relaxed state, the brain produces **alpha waves**, which are relatively slow and regular. Once asleep, **Stage 1** begins, characterized by slower breathing, and irregular, relatively erratic brain waves. During the five minutes in this stage, **hypnogogic** ("having to do with drowsiness") sensations like falling or floating may be experienced. Alpha waves cease and are replaced by slower theta waves. **Stage 2** lasts about 20 minutes and involves deeper relaxation and occasional bursts of rhythmic brainwaves called **sleep spindles** and K-complexes. As **Stage 3** begins the brain starts to produce **delta waves** which appear, on an EEG monitor, as large, slow waves. Stage 3 is a transition into **Stage 4**, which involves stronger, more consistent delta waves. These two stages together are referred to as **slow-wave sleep**, last about 30 minutes, and are the most difficult from which to wake one.

About an hour after falling asleep, individuals begin to move back into Stage 3 and then Stage 2. But, instead of sliding back into Stage 1 sleep, people typically move into a 10-minute period of **REM** (rapid eye movement) sleep. In REM, brain waves are similar to what they were in Stage 1, but breathing is more rapid and irregular, heart rate increases, and the eyes dart back and forth (underneath closed eyelids). It's usually during REM sleep that people dream. These dreams are prevented from being acted out because the brainstem blocks messages from the motor cortex, which leaves the body more or less paralyzed. REM sleep is, in fact, sometimes called **paradoxical sleep** because the sleeper appears calm and relaxed despite a great deal of cortical activity. After the REM stage, the sleeper moves back into Stage 2 and the next cycle continues. With each cycle, however, periods of REM sleep get longer and periods of Stage 4 sleep get shorter.

SLEEP DISORDERS

Several sleep disorders can interfere with this typical sleep pattern. **Insomnia** involves recurring difficulty in falling asleep or staying asleep. **Narcolepsy** is characterized by sudden and uncontrollable attacks of sleep during waking hours. In some cases, the narcoleptic may fall directly into REM sleep, completely losing muscular tension. People suffering from **sleep apnea** stop breathing intermittently during sleep; the lack of oxygen then wakes the sleeper up enough to be able to snort for more air. These brief episodes can occur hundreds of times in a night.

These sorts of sleep problems underscore the fact that people need to sleep and, perhaps, need to dream. It is thought that sleep itself might be necessary for restoring brain and body tissues, consolidating memories, and releasing the growth hormone from the pituitary gland, although these explanations are still speculative.

DREAMS

Dreaming, too, hasn't been conclusively explained, but not for lack of trying. Freud saw dreams as a way to preserve sleep: The **manifest content** of the dream (the images that actually appear to the dreamer) is a disguised version of the dream's **latent content** (usually a "forbidden" sexual or aggressive wish that the dreamer would repress if awake). By distorting or disguising the wish, the dreamer avoids the anxiety that would accompany his being aware of it and, therefore, can remain asleep.

Other explanations focus on dreams' physiological functions. For example, it is thought that dreams might stimulate the brain, which might then help to build and maintain neural connections. Or, according to **activation-synthesis theory**, the brain's neurons fire randomly during sleep, and as we awake, we construct a dream in order to make sense out of the random images that have been generated.

Information-processing explanations claim that dreams are a way to consolidate information. As we dream, we sort through the day's events and stamp them into memory.

In any case, REM sleep and the dreams that accompany it appear to be necessary. When deprived of this for a period of time, people typically make up for it later by experiencing prolonged periods of REM sleep (referred to as **REM rebound**).

ALTERED STATES OF CONSCIOUSNESS

Hypnosis is an induced state of consciousness characterized by deep relaxation and heightened suggestibility. However, there is no evidence that someone who is hypnotized will do things he or she wouldn't do if he/she were not under hypnosis.

One explanation for the effects of hypnosis, then, is that it is simply a heightened state of motivation. According to this view, people who are hypnotized want to be hypnotized and want to do what the hypnotist tells them to do. A related explanation is that hypnotized subjects are fulfilling **social roles** by behaving the way they think the hypnotist wants them to behave. And, finally, others claim that hypnosis involves **dissociation**—a split in consciousness, which allows the person to become aware of his or her activities while under hypnosis.

Psychoactive drugs produce a state of consciousness that is different from "normal" consciousness by mimicking, inhibiting, or stimulating the activity of neurotransmitters. The three most common types of these drugs are **depressants** (which slow down body functions and neurological activity), **stimulants** (which increase neural activity and body functions), and **hallucinogens** (which distort perceptions and produce sensations that have no physical basis).

Depressants include **alcohol**, **barbiturates**, and **opiates**. Small amounts of alcohol, for example, are relaxing because they slow down the sympathetic nervous system. People may become more aggressive, daring, or outgoing when drinking, but that occurs because the alcohol slows down brain activity that controls inhibitions—not because alcohol is a stimulant.

CHAPTER 6

Learning

Chapter 6

LEARNING

Learning is typically defined as a relatively enduring change in behavior that is the product of experience. "Experience" might best be thought of as past experience: earlier events that influence the way an organism behaves in the present. Traditionally, that would mean that learning involves the effects of various **stimuli** (environmental events that are capable of triggering **responses** (changes in behavior). This idea is credited to the **behaviorists**, who first began studying learning and wanted to focus only on observable events. More recent explanations of learning, though, also take into account **cognitive factors**, including expectations and the ability to represent events mentally. There are two types of learning—associative and non-associative—and three distinct procedures for producing associative learning: classical conditioning, operant conditioning, and observational learning.

NON-ASSOCIATIVE LEARNING

Non-associative learning occurs when the repeated presentation of a single stimulus produces an enduring change in behavior. In the case of **habituation**, for example, repeated presentations of a stimulus eventually reduce responses to that stimulus. If, for example, a clock chimes every 15 minutes, or a neighbor's dog barks frequently, or noisy traffic regularly passes, one is likely to stop attending to those stimuli. **Sensitization** occurs when the repeated or long-lasting presentation of an intense stimulus increases the response to a weaker stimulus; while watching a movie, the sound of someone being slapped might not ordinarily be enough to startle you, but if there had first been a long, noisy, intense fight scene, followed by a brief pause, the sound of that slap might scare you.

ASSOCIATIVE LEARNING

Associative learning involves the learning of a connection either between two stimuli (as in classical conditioning) or between a response and a stimulus (as in operant conditioning).

Classical Conditioning. **Classical conditioning** (or **Pavlovian conditioning**) produces changes in responding by pairing two stimuli together. One of those stimuli (the **unconditioned stimulus**, or **US**) already produces the response of interest (the **unconditioned response**, or **UR**). Meat powder, for example, would automatically make any dog salivate (as in the famous case of Pavlov's dogs). By repeatedly presenting meat powder (the US) immediately after presenting another stimulus (a **neutral stimulus**—one that wouldn't automatically produce the UR—such as a bell), the neutral stimulus becomes capable of producing the response. At this point, then, the neutral stimulus is called a **conditioned stimulus** (CS) and the response it now produces (in this case, salivation) is called the **conditioned response** (CR.) This basic procedure is depicted in Figure 6.1.

Before conditioning:

US ⟶ UR

(food)   (salivating)

The first trial:

neutral stimulus   +   US ⟶ UR

(bell)   (food) (salivating)
⟶ no salivating

After learning has occurred:

CS ⟶ CR

(bell)   (salivating)

Figure 6.1: The basic classical conditioning procedure.

It is now widely accepted that what an organism learns manifests itself as an **expectation** that the US will show up after the CS. Thus, conditioned responses can virtually always be thought of as "preparatory" responses: They prepare an organism for the unconditioned stimulus (and the inevitable unconditioned response) that predictably shows up after the conditioned stimulus. If meat powder predictably follows the ringing of a bell, a dog might just as well start salivating when the bell rings. If the CS is repeatedly presented without the US, the CR will go away. This is referred to as **extinction**, and can be explained as the learning of a new expectation: that the US no longer follows the CS.

Operant Conditioning. **Operant conditioning** involves learning an association between a stimulus and a response that follows it (predictably). Learning this association will either increase or decrease the frequency of the response, depending on the quality of the stimulus (pleasant or unpleasant). In other words, the consequences of a behavior affect how often it will be performed (the term "operant" refers to the fact that the behavior "operates" on the environment, making something happen; this is also called **instrumental conditioning** because the response is "instrumental" in making a stimulus occur). There are two types of consequences, and two ways in which each one can come about. Table 6.1 summarizes these consequences.

Table 6.1: The four consequences involved in operant conditioning.

	Behavior Increases	**Behavior Decreases**
Stimulus Applied	Positive Reinforcement	Positive Punishment
Stimulus Removed	Negative Reinforcement	Negative Punishment

Reinforcement always involves an increase in the target behavior. The words "positive" and "negative" refer to what's happening with a stimulus: either it shows up (positive) or is removed (negative). Thus **positive reinforcement** involves presenting a stimulus (e.g., giving a dog a treat after it stands on its hind legs) and **negative reinforcement** involves removing a stimulus (e.g., a headache going away after taking aspirin). In either case, adding or removing a stimulus produces a desirable effect and, so, the behavior will happen more often (yes, negative reinforcement *increases* the frequency of behaviors).

Punishment *always* involves a decrease in the target behavior. For obscure reasons, punishment isn't usually referred to as "positive" or "negative," though. What might be considered "positive punishment" (e.g., yanking on a dog's choke collar when it barks) and "negative punishment" (e.g., paying a fine—that is, losing money—after getting caught for speeding) are both generally referred to simply as **punishment** (although the latter is sometimes called **response-cost training**). It is important to remember that positive and negative punishment do not refer to "good," "bad," "pleasant," or "unpleasant." Positive indicates that a stimulus was applied and negative means that a stimulus was removed.

Not only does the type of consequence that might follow a behavior influence how it changes, the way in which that consequence is doled out influences it, too. Usually this is discussed in terms of **reinforcement schedules**—rules for determining when reinforcement will be given. The four basic schedules differ in whether presentations of a reinforcer will be determined by how many times a response has been made (a **ratio schedule**) or the amount of time since the last reinforcement (an **interval schedule**), and whether the ratio or interval is **fixed** or **variable**. On a **fixed ratio** schedule, then, a rat might receive a pellet of food for every sixth lever press, whereas on a **variable ratio** schedule the *average* number of presses required for food would be six (or eight, or 132. . .whatever the schedule dictates). On a **fixed interval** schedule, a food reinforcer would become available, say, six seconds after the last reinforcer was delivered; the first response after that six-second interval, then, would produce the food. That is, the rat would not receive food for pressing the lever before that six seconds was up, but would get reinforced for the first lever press after the six seconds was up. On a **variable interval** schedule, the amount of time between getting a reinforcer and the next one becoming available keeps changing (although, again, it can be described in terms of some average interval).

As with classical conditioning, **extinction** happens for operantly conditioned behaviors when a stimulus that used to show up predictably doesn't appear any more. In this case, though, that stimulus is a reinforcer or punisher and the learned behavior doesn't necessarily disappear, as it does in classical conditioning, but returns to its **baseline level** (the frequency with which it happened prior to conditioning).

Operant conditioning and classical conditioning can often be hard to distinguish. Table 6.2 lists a few ways to tell the two apart.

Table 6.2: Differences Between Classical Conditioning and Operant Conditioning.

	Classical Conditioning	Operant Conditioning
Type of Behavior:	reflexive, elicited	voluntary, emitted
Learning Process:	pair two stimuli; CS + US; stimuli appear regardless of learner's behavior	pair response with stimulus (consequence); behavior & consequence; stimuli appear because of learner's behavior
Evidence of Learning:	a stimulus (CS) produces a new response (CR)	a behavior happens more or less often

Observational Learning. The idea behind **observational learning** is that we can learn operant behaviors (and maybe reflexive, classically conditioned ones) indirectly. That is, we personally don't need to be reinforced or punished for something in order to do it more or less often; we can learn what the consequences are by watching them happen to other people and then apply what we've learned to our own lives. The people from whom we learn are called **models**. The ability to learn **vicariously** (by watching what happens to models) exponentially expands the opportunities for learning.

CHAPTER 7

Cognition

Chapter 7

COGNITION

Cognition can be thought of as the mental activities involved in solving problems: thinking, language, memory, and intelligence.

THINKING

A variety of thought processes either facilitate or impede problem solving. For example, people often use shortcuts called **heuristics** (mental rules-of-thumb) as a way to solve problems—especially those involving estimates of "likelihood"—with minimal effort. For instance, if you want to decide how likely it is that a course you could sign up for would be interesting, you might compare its characteristics (e.g., who's teaching it, what department is offering it, whether there are lab sections with it) to those of other courses you've liked. The closer the fit, the more likely you would expect the course to be interesting. This problem-solving method is called the **representativeness heuristic**: You're asking yourself how similar or "representative" one event (e.g., the course you might want to take) is of a class of events (e.g., courses you like). Another shortcut, the **availability heuristic**, involves judging the likelihood that an event will happen in terms of how readily you can bring an instance of it to mind. Events that are more vivid or that have happened more recently would be judged as being more likely to happen than those that are less vivid or recent. Thus, based on "availability," you might come to the conclusion that judicial trials are relatively common and plea bargains relatively rare, when the reverse is actually true: News reports of trials tend to be more sensational, and so more memorable, than reports of plea bargains. Neither of these heuristics necessarily steers you toward a correct judgment, although it probably frequently does.

Much of what is studied with respect to thinking and problem-solving is, in fact, the ways in which people systematically and predictably make errors in their judgments. For instance, the term **confirmation bias** refers to people's tendency to look for information that will support their beliefs: If you expect a movie to be good, you might make note of the fine acting and ignore the bad story line. **Functional fixedness** is the inability to see new uses for familiar objects: Unable to find your screwdriver, you may not recognize that a quarter would work just as well.

LANGUAGE

Language, too, solves a problem: how to get ideas from one person to another. To make that possible, languages use systems of rules (i.e., **grammar**) that allow everyone using the language to make sense out of it in the same way. The two most-studied systems of linguistic rules are **semantics**, rules for mapping **morphemes** (words, or parts of words, that convey meaning) onto the ideas they represent, and **syntax**, rules for combining morphemes in meaningful ways. Skill in using these rules develops with age, of course, although age-related changes in speaking are usually described in terms of the number of words a child can string together. At about four to six months of age, babies enter a **babbling stage** during which they appear to be practicing the sounds used in their language. This stage lasts roughly until the child's first birthday. During this time, their ability to recognize sounds that aren't used in their language increases and the occurrence of such sounds decreases. At about a year of age, children enter the **one-word stage**, which lasts until about 18 months. Although speaking only one word at a time, accompanying gestures convey additional meaning (e.g., saying "Cup" while reaching toward a cup might mean, "Hand me that cup"). This is called **telegraphic speech**, and is also typical of the **two-word stage**, during which children primarily use a noun combined with a verb (e.g., "Doggie bite") or, a few months later, an adjective followed by a noun (e.g., "Bad doggie").

Although attempts have been made to explain language development in terms of operant conditioning principles, one most notably made by **B. F. Skinner**, conditioning probably can't account for how quickly children learn language and the novel ways in which they use it (e.g., making grammatical mistakes they could never have heard anyone else make). **Noam Chomsky** has claimed that children have a **language acquisition device**—a universal, built-in mental system that steers us toward interpreting and using language in particular ways. Others have proposed that the neuronal complexity of our brains allows children to analyze their experiences with language statistically and thereby determine which word orders are acceptable, which sounds are likely to go together, which meaning of a word applies given a specific context ("down" as a direction versus "down" as a state of mind), and so forth.

MEMORY

Of course, without **memory**—the ability to store information and retrieve it again—thinking and language would be useless. Memory is typically divided into three types: Sensory, short-term, and long-term. A great deal of research and theory in this area is devoted to figuring out how information gets from one type of memory to another and how people get the information back out of storage.

Sensory memory is a fleeting awareness of whatever the senses have detected. If attended to, this information enters **short-term memory**, also called **working memory** because it's the information that can be kept in the mind long enough to solve problems. This information will be lost unless extra effort is expended to transfer it to **long-term memory** (an unlimited, and perhaps permanent, storehouse of memories). **Mnemonic strategies** are deliberate, though sometimes automatic and unconscious, methods used for getting information into long-term memory (or keeping more information in short-term memory). For instance, **rehearsal** involves the deliberate, conscious repetition of information) and **chunking** involves grouping pieces of information into meaningful units, as when you combine the numbers "5-7-3" into a single area code or the words "Internal Revenue Service" into the acronym "IRS."

INTELLIGENCE

Remembering, using language, thinking, and other psychological processes allow you to solve problems. **Intelligence** is about how well you solve problems. From a psychological perspective, defining it this way begs three major questions: First, how can the ability to solve problems be summed up in a single score that can be used to predict other behaviors and characteristics? Second, since there are different kinds of problems to solve, are there also different kinds of intelligence? And, third, why do people differ in their problem-solving abilities?

Alfred Binet was the first to develop an intelligence test: a battery of questions about topics typically covered in (French) schools. This test yielded a score that reflected the test-taker's **mental age** (the chronological age that corresponds to a given level of performance on the test). If an 8-year-old gets the same score as the average 10-year-old, his/her mental age is 10. Eventually, this measure of intelligence was incorporated into the **intelligence quotient (IQ)**: mental age divided by chronological age, multiplied by 100 (to eliminate the decimal point). An 8-year-old with a mental age of 10 would have an IQ of 125. Of course, a 30-year-old who scored as well as the average 60-year-old would have an IQ of 200, which doesn't make much sense. Therefore, IQ scores (as they're still loosely called) are based on a comparison between the test-taker's score and the average score for others of his or her age (this is called **standardization** or **norms-based referencing**). By design, and statistical manipulations, the average "IQ score" for contemporary intelligence tests is made to be 100.

Tests that generate a single IQ score assume that there is a single, unitary skill underlying people's ability to solve all sorts of problems. Early in the last century, **Charles Spearman** labeled this general intelligence "g". Most who study intelligence these days, though, subscribe to the idea that there are **multiple intelligences**—separate, distinct problem-solving abilities. The ability to perform well on math problems (an aspect of analytical intelligence), for example, doesn't guarantee that you'll be able to work out problems in your personal relationships (an aspect of practical intelligence); these two types of problems require different skills to solve them.

Nature vs. Nurture. People differ in how much of any particular kind of intelligence they seem to possess. Why? The answer is usually placed in the context of the **nature vs. nurture** debate. "Nature" refers to our biological, genetic heritage, whereas "nurture" refers to environmental effects on our development. It's clear that both contribute to differences in intelligence. Where genetic similarity can be determined, as with genetically identical twins, pairs of siblings, and parent-child pairs, the more alike people are genetically, the more similar their IQ scores are (supporting the idea that nature influences differences in intelligence). However, identical twins raised apart are less alike than identical twins raised together (supporting the idea that nurture influences differences in intelligence). As with so many other characteristics, it's probably the case that differences in IQ scores are the product of an **interaction** between nature and nurture. For example, those who are "built" by nature to be smart should benefit more from a stimulating environment than those who are not. The interaction means that not everyone who's built to be smart would be equally smart (due to differing environments), and not everyone in a stimulating environment would be equally smart (due to different genetic make-ups). This general principle—that nature and nurture interact to influence development—can be applied to most psychological phenomena.

CHAPTER 8

Motivation
and Emotion

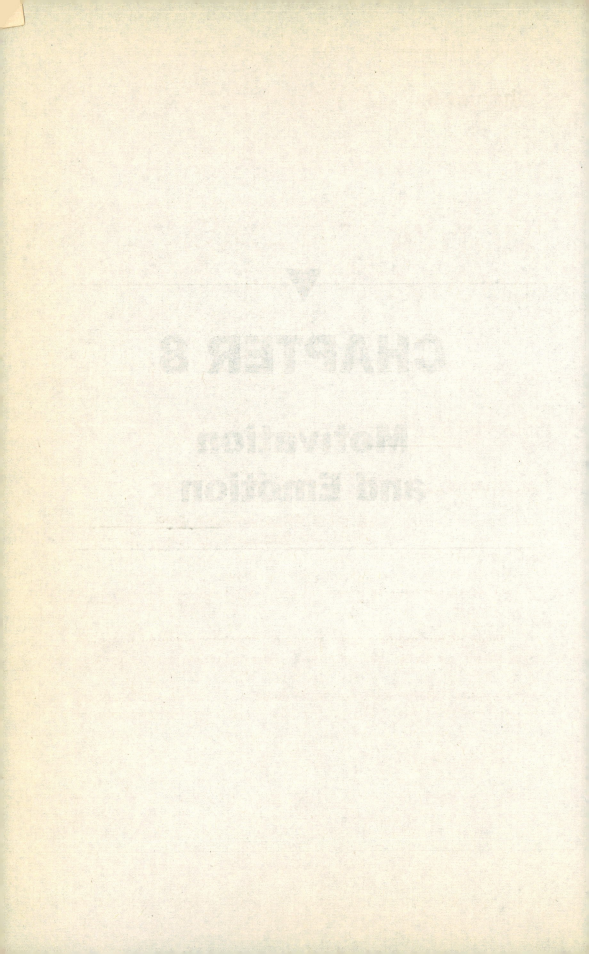

Chapter 8

MOTIVATION AND EMOTION

The topics of motivation and emotion belong together: Emotions can be thought of as a running commentary on how well the needs and desires that we call "motivation" are being fulfilled. Emotions also generate motives (to hit other people, be with other people, stay away from people, etc.), so the influence goes both ways.

MOTIVATION

Motivation can be defined as the psychological process that energizes and directs behavior. Needs and desires may both fuel our behavior, but needs and desires aren't necessarily the same thing (e.g., we can desire something we don't need). The word "motivation," then, describes what these two things have in common: activating behavior and steering it toward a goal.

Many of our motives serve biological functions—getting food, getting water, reproducing, and so forth. Other important motives seem to serve primarily social-psychological goals: affiliation, achievement, and maintaining a favorable self-image, to name a few. But regardless of the specific functions they serve, motives are typically explained in terms of both biological and social-psychological influences.

Hunger. **Hunger** is often used to illustrate how these factors can impact the occurrence and expression of a motive. Oddly, no one can yet say for sure from where the experience of hunger comes, but a number of things do clearly influence it. One of those is **glucose** (blood sugar that provides energy for bodily functions), and one source of glucose is the breakdown of foods that have recently been eaten (see Figure 8.1). As a general rule, then, people and animals are more likely to eat when glucose levels are low (indicating that they haven't had food for a while). However, high levels of glucose in the blood trigger the release of **insulin** (a hormone produced in the pancreas), and insulin converts glucose to stored fat, removing it from the blood stream. It's not entirely clear, then, whether hunger would be triggered by low glucose levels, high insulin levels, or both.

food (containing sugars)

⟶ digestion

⟶ sugars released, as glucose, into the blood

⟶ release of insulin

⟶ increased insulin, reduced glucose

⟶ hunger

⟶ food...

Figure 8.1: The interaction of glucose and insulin.

It's likely that these chemicals influence hunger because of signals sent to the brain regarding their levels in the blood. The part of the brain that seems to be most important for monitoring hunger-related signals is the **hypothalamus**. Specifically, the **ventromedial hypothalamus (VH;** the lower middle portion of the hypothalamus) appears to be responsible for stopping hunger: stimulation to it will depress hunger, and damage to it results in eating even when one is full. On the other hand, the **lateral hypothalamus (LH**; the sides of the hypothalamus) is responsible for increasing hunger: stimulation causes eating even among animals that are well-fed, and damage to it will prevent even an animal that's starving from eating food.

In addition to these factors, each of us appears to have a **set point**—the weight our own body works to maintain. When weight drops below the set point, hunger increases (resulting in the intake of extra calories) and activity level decreases (one becomes lethargic, and therefore burns fewer calories), resulting in an increase in weight. When weight rises above the set point, hunger decreases (resulting in the intake of fewer calories) and the activity level increases (causing the burning of more calories), resulting in a drop in weight.

But hunger and eating aren't regulated by biological factors alone. Social-psychological factors, such as ideals for beauty and the type of cues that trigger eating, also influence when or how much people eat. As examples, two eating disorders—**anorexia nervosa** and **bulimia**—appear to stem in part from adolescent girls' desire to achieve an ideal of being slender (boys typically increase activity to lose weight, rather than changing eating habits). Anorexics are obsessed with food but avoid eating it. As a result, they often drop far below normal body weight. Bulimics, too, are concerned with body image and typically are dieters, but they **binge and purge** on a regular basis, eating large amounts of food at a single sitting (i.e., binging) and then using laxatives, diuretics, or vomiting to get rid of it again (purging).

Another psychological influence on the motivation to eat is a personality trait called "externality." People who are **externals** become hungry when external cues—like the smell of food or the time of day—tell them to eat. **Internals**, on the other hand, rely on bodily cues like hunger pangs and levels of glucose or insulin in the blood. Externals are more likely to be overweight and engage in dieting.

EMOTIONS

Emotions prepare us to deal with the many ways in which events can impact our motives, goals, values, and so forth. To follow through on the hunger example, you might feel guilty or depressed if you ate when you didn't want to eat, or you might be happy if you ate when you did want to. Also, emotions are a source of motivation in themselves. This is manifested when you stay away from things that will make you feel bad and seek out things that will make you feel good.

There's fairly wide agreement that some subset of emotions (**basic-level emotions**; e.g., anger, sadness, joy, fear, and love) is wired into our nervous systems, whereas others are either combinations of the basic-level emotions (**blended emotions**) or learned. All emotions presumably involve some sort of **physiological arousal** (e.g., an increase or decrease in heart rate), **behavioral expression** (running or punching), and **conscious experience** ("I feel agitated!"). Different theories of emotion have described these components as interacting in different ways.

According to the **Cannon-Bard theory**, perceiving a stimulus that has relevance to one's well-being will generate arousal and a subjective emotional experience simultaneously; information about the stimulus is sent to both the sympathetic nervous system (thus the arousal) and the cortex (resulting in the subjective experience) at the same time (see Figure

8.2). For example, if my neighbor's dog growls menacingly at me, my heart rate increases and I realize that I'm afraid. Neither causes the other. But according to the **James-Lange theory**, the perception of a stimulus causes arousal first, which then causes me to feel an emotion. I'm afraid because I can feel my heart pounding and my legs running. Without the arousal, I wouldn't be afraid. One implication of this idea is called the **facial feedback hypothesis**: The activity of facial muscles tells us whether we're happy or not. In fact, people asked to hold a pen in their teeth (which activates muscles involved in smiling) report finding cartoons to be funnier than people asked to hold a pen with their lips (which activates muscles involved in frowning).

A third theory of emotion, Stanley Schacter's **two-factor theory**, says that the quality of an emotional experience (Is it anger? Fear? Jealousy?) depends on how arousal is labeled. Schacter thought that arousal was the same physiologically, regardless of which emotion we might experience. What makes one emotional experience different from another is the decision to call it one emotion rather than another. For example, if you decide that you're aroused because someone insulted you, you become angry; if instead you think that same arousal was due to your attraction to someone, you fall in love. One finding consistent with these ideas is that people whose levels of arousal are increased through exercise, or other means, become more angry when insulted than people who haven't been made physiologically aroused first. This is called **excitation transfer**.

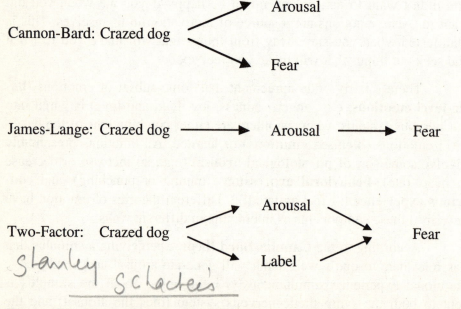

Figure 8.2: Three theories of emotion.

CHAPTER 9

Development

Chapter 9

DEVELOPMENT

The field of **developmental psychology** deals with systematic, predictable changes in thinking and behavior over the lifespan. Because the focus is on how people change over long periods of time, correlational studies and experiments (discussed in Chapter 1) aren't always the best way to conduct research on development. Two other types of studies do allow researchers to make inferences about how people change with age.

DEVELOPMENTAL RESEARCH METHODS

Cross-sectional studies involve comparing people of different ages at the same point in time. To see whether people become more politically conservative with age, for example, one might administer some sort of "political ideology" test to a group of 20-year-olds, a group of 30-year-olds, a group of 40-year-olds, and so forth, and then compare the levels of conservatism across those groups. If 70-year-olds have higher scores than 30-year-olds, you might then conclude that conservatism increases with age. The major problem with cross-sectional studies, though, is that age is confounded with cohort. A cohort is a group of people born during the same period of time (e.g., during the 1960s or 1970s). If age and cohort are "confounded," this means that it cannot be determined whether differences across age groups are due to changes in age itself, or to differences in the periods of time during which the subjects grew up. Differences in conservatism, for example, could mean that something about growing older causes people to become more conservative, or that older people grew up at a time when conservatism was encouraged (and so would have gotten the same conservatism scores even when they were 30 years old) and that younger people grew up at a time when being liberal was encouraged.

That particular type of confounding problem is solved in **longitudinal** studies, which involve tracking the behavior of a single cohort over a long period of time. Using the conservatism example, the political ideologies of a group of 30-year-olds might be tested now, and then again in 40 years, when the subjects are 70. Sounds good, but in this case, age is confounded with time of testing; it cannot be determined whether differences across age groups are due to changes in age itself, or to differences in the periods of time during which the subjects took the test. Again, differences in conservatism scores could mean that something about growing older causes people to become more conservative, or that the political climate itself grew more conservative as these people approached age 70 (meaning that differences across age groups weren't caused by these people getting older). Also, in longitudinal research, studies often lose participants due to life circumstances (deaths, a move, etc.), which present a threat to the validity of the studies' conclusions. Ideally then, a **cross-sequential study** can be implemented, in which people of different ages (as in a cross-sectional study) are followed over a long period of time (as in a longitudinal study). This would allow one to determine whether differences across age groups have to do with getting older, with cohorts, or with the time of testing.

PIAGET'S THEORY OF COGNITIVE DEVELOPMENT

Theories of development usually deal with changes over time in a particular area of psychological functioning; thus there are theories of social development, moral development, personality development, and so on. **Piaget's** theory of cognitive development, for example, describes how children's thinking (their ability to solve problems) changes as they get older. According to Piaget, during the **sensorimotor stage**, children think only in terms of what they can sense and what they can do with what they sense. Among other things, this means that young children don't have **object permanence**, the understanding that objects continue to exist even when their presence can't be sensed. If a blanket is thrown over an eight-month-old child's favorite ball, the child won't pull the blanket off and get the ball, even though the child is capable of that behavior; the child acts as if the ball no longer exists.

Stage	Age	Cognitive Skills
Sensorimotor	0 - 2 years	lacks concept of object permanence; knows what it can do with what it senses
Pre-Operational	2 - 6 years	understands object permanence; thinks symbolically (e.g., uses language); highly egocentric; logic is intuitive and dominated by perception; can't conserve
Concrete Operations	6 - 12 years	acquires conservation; generates and applies logical rules for concrete problems
Formal Operations	12+ years	thinks scientifically; thinks hypothetically about abstractions

Table 9.1: Piaget's Stages of Cognitive Development.

When children develop the concept of object permanence, they enter the **pre-operational stage** (about two years to six or seven years). An "operation" is a logical thought; according to Piaget, children at this age don't use logical reasoning, but instead reason intuitively. For children within the pre-operational stage, the world is whatever it appears to be. As an example, young children have trouble solving problems that require **conservation**—the understanding that some quantitative aspects of objects (e.g., mass, volume, weight, number) don't change just because the object's appearance has been transformed in some way. A hot dog that has been cut into five pieces is thought to be more hot dog than one that has been cut into four pieces; juice in a tall, narrow glass is thought of as more juice than is the same amount of juice in a short, fat glass. If it looks as though there's more, there's more, even though logically (from our adult perspective) there isn't. Children at this stage are also especially **egocentric**—they have trouble seeing things from other people's perspectives. If they can't see you, you can't see them; if they want a teddy bear for their birthday, you must want a teddy bear for yours.

From about six or seven years to eleven or twelve years, children are in the **concrete operational stage**. They now think logically (that is, use logical rules consistently), but only about things that are "concrete"—things with which they've had direct experience or can easily imagine, not about things that are abstract. They can solve conservation problems, but have trouble understanding algebra (which would require them to think about numbers they can't see, and which change from one algebra problem to the next: sometimes x is 13, and sometimes x is 4).

At around 12 years, children become capable of **formal operational** thinking, or the logic of science. They can now think abstractly, applying logical rules to envision things they haven't seen. This allows them to understand that many factors could influence the behavior being measured in an experiment, regardless of whether they know what those factors are, and that random assignment to control and experimental groups would necessarily eliminate all but one of them even though, again, they don't even know what the factors are.

According to Piaget, changes in children's understanding of the world are the product of **disequilibrium**: A child understands the world in one particular way and then sees something happen that can't fit into that understanding. In order to make sense out of what has happened, the child has to change the way he or she understands the world. In terms of the conservation problem used earlier, a child might have a **scheme**—an understanding of how some aspect of the world works—about "quantity" or "mass" that says, "Things are the way they appear" (if it looks the same, it's the same and if it looks like more, it's more). When she picks one hot dog up in each hand, they seem to weigh the same amount, so she assimilates that experience into her scheme (**assimilation** involves understanding events in terms of your current scheme). This is just another instance of things that look the same being the same, and this time the things are hot dogs. But when Dad then cuts one of those hot dogs into four pieces and the other into five, so that it looks like there's more of one than the other, it can't fit into her scheme: She already knows there's the same amount of food in each hot dog. Enough of these experiences with disequilibrium and she'll be forced to **accommodate**—change her understanding of mass (in this case) to more accurately reflect the way the world works. In this case, that means changing her scheme to include the idea that mass stays the same unless something is added or taken away, which demonstrates a **logical rule**.

ERIKSON'S THEORY OF PSYCHO-SOCIAL DEVELOPMENT

Erikson's theory of **psycho-social development** also relies heavily on the idea that tension (or disequilibrium) is necessary for change. According to Erikson, people go through a series of eight stages in their lives, each of which involves a different **crisis**. These crises are listed below in Table 9.2. The first five crises involve conflicts between what a child can do, and what others in his or her environment will allow him or her do. A preschooler, for example, is capable of coming up with plans and carrying them out (i.e., **initiative**), but parents inevitably try to squelch some of that initiative by instilling a conscience in the child that, at appropriate times, makes the child feel **guilt**. How the child resolves this tension between what others want from him and what he or she can do determines what his personality will be like later on. In this case, it determines whether the child grows up to be purposeful, paralyzed by guilt, or somewhere in between.

The last few crises involve conflicts within one's self. In middle adulthood, for example, people struggle with choices between sharing their wisdom and experience with other people (**generativity**) and taking care of only their own deteriorating physical and mental abilities (**stagnation**).

Crisis	Age	Source of Tension
Trust vs. Mistrust	0 - 1 years	Dependence on others; Are others reliable?
Autonomy vs. Doubt and Shame	1 - 3 years	capable of self-control; allowed to exercise it?
Initiative vs. Guilt	3 - 5 years	can set goals; is that encouraged?
Industry vs. Inferiority	6 - 11 years	can reason, likes success; praised and taught?
Identity vs. Role Confusion	12 - 18 years	can reflect on identity and consider multiple roles; willing to make an effort to integrate all those roles?

Crisis	Age	Source of Tension
Intimacy vs. Isolation	18 - 35 years	ready to break away from family and form new intimate relationships; willing to share yourself?
Generativity vs. Stagnation	36 - 55 years	kids are gone—you're free; show interest in others?
Integrity vs. Despair	55+ years	reflecting on your life; accept it all?

Table 9.2: Erikson's Eight Psycho-Social Stages.

CHAPTER 10

Personality

Chapter 10

PERSONALITY

THE PSYCHOANALYTIC APPROACH

Psychoanalytic, social-cognitive, and humanistic theories are three major areas of focus within the study of personality. **Psychoanalytic theories** (e.g., Freud, Jung, Adler, Horney, Erikson) share the common beliefs that people's behavior is motivated largely by unconscious needs; that people feel conflict between getting those needs met, on the one hand, and social pressures to behave in ways that wouldn't meet those needs, on the other; and that maladaptive, unhealthy behavior is the product of that conflict.

The Motives Behind Behavior. Sigmund **Freud's** theory of **psychoanalysis**, for example, describes people as having two fundamental needs or motives: **sex** and **aggression**. Unbridled sex and aggression are not generally accepted among the general population, so there are social pressures on children (from parents, in large part, who represent society as a whole) to restrain themselves from acting on these needs. A child's personality develops as it figures out how to get its basic needs met while still making Mom and Dad happy.

The Structure and Dynamics of Personality. In order to account for the sorts of behaviors he saw in his patients, though, Freud had much more to say than that about personality development. First, he saw personality as having three components—id, ego, and superego—each of which is essentially a different way of thinking, feeling, and behaving. The term **id** refers to the biological part of our personality and, so, to the built-in sexual and aggressive needs that drive our behavior. (It should be pointed out that Freud thought of just about anything that feels good as sexual, including things like urinating, defecating, and other bodily functions.) Infants are pure id: They express their needs—act on impulses—without restraint. To put it another way, they operate according to **the pleasure**

principle: Do what feels good, and do it now. But a baby is a baby, so its needs aren't necessarily going to get met through impulsive behavior (e.g., it might cry impulsively when it feels hunger pangs, but that doesn't guarantee that food will show up). As a result of this frustration (and physical maturation), it begins to think about how to get its needs met in the environment it's in. This is what **ego**, the rational, realistic part of our personality, is about. Ego involves learning, problem-solving, and reasoning, or operating according to **the reality principle**: Do what will get your needs met effectively, efficiently, and without getting yourself hurt. Of course, part of reality is the parent's ideas about right and wrong. As the child gets punished and rewarded for various activities, it distills rules for "appropriate" behavior. These rules are the basis for **superego**, the social part of our personality that allows us to get along with other people. The child's behavior and thinking can now operate according to a third principle, **the morality principle**: Do what's right, and don't do what's wrong.

Conflict and Anxiety. These three principles, which tell the child, and later the adult, how to behave (impulsively, realistically, or morally), can come into conflict. For example, the child might have an urge for a candy bar (id), come up with a plan to take one from his little sister (ego), and know that stealing it would be wrong (superego). When there is conflict over how to behave (i.e., tension), there is **anxiety**. Nobody likes feeling anxious, or fearful, so something has to be done to get rid of the feeling. Although people can take realistic and effective steps to deal with anxiety, that's not nearly as interesting as what they do to avoid dealing with the anxiety. In the case of **phobias**, people develop intense and irrational fears of objects. From the Freudian perspective, these objects are symbolic or metaphorical reminders of things the person wants, but can't allow himself/herself to have. The phobia keeps him away from the object and, so, keeps the anxiety from popping up. In the case of **defense mechanisms**, people distort reality in order to delude themselves into believing that something anxiety-provoking isn't happening.

Psychosexual Stages. But Freud was even more specific than that about how the major conflicts originate. He saw personality developing through **psychosexual stages**—periods of life defined by parts of the body that do the most to make you feel good. What makes these parts of the body feel so good is that they also involve the most tension, and getting rid of tension feels good. During the **oral stage** (birth to about 2 years), most of children's needs are met quickly, but parents inevitably put them on some sort of feeding schedule. There's also pain to endure when new teeth come in. This means children experience a lot of tension having to do with using their mouths, throats, and the entire digestive tract (i.e., the **oral zone**). If it's a moderate amount of tension, a child can figure out how to deal with it effectively (developing his ego in the process). But too little tension results in the child not developing his ego and too much tension results in compulsive behavior aimed at trying to get the need met or avoiding anxiety about not getting the needs met. In either case, the child is said to have developed a **fixation**—a desire to build his life around getting certain needs met (oral ones, in this example). As he or she is growing up, an orally fixated child must find ways of getting oral needs met that are age-appropriate, won't aggravate other people, and won't interfere too much with the rest of his or her life. Thus they do things that symbolically meet their oral needs: chewing gum, smoking, or biting fingernails, as examples.

During the **anal stage** (roughly two to four years), children come into conflict with parents over toilet training. Parents often want the child to endure tension by resisting the urge to defecate or to sacrifice pleasure by defecating before tension has built up. Again, a moderate amount of tension arising over this fight for control of the child's bowel movements is good (it helps ego develop), but too much or too little results in a fixation. Anally fixated people come in two types. **Anal retentive** people put off getting pleasure until the last moment and like to have everything in its proper place. **Anal expulsive** people are messy and rebellious.

At about four years of age, children enter the **phallic stage**. How this stage plays out depends on whether the child is a boy or a girl. Boys wake up one day and realize they have a penis and that it feels good. They also realize they feel a sexual attraction toward Mom; an awkward position to be in, given that Dad already has Mom, might get angry about the possible competition, and is big enough to do something about it (possibly by taking away the boy's penis). The boy now feels **castration anxiety**. This scenario is referred to as the **Oedipus complex** or **Oedipal conflict**. Ideally, the boy resolves it by giving up on Mom and **identifying** with Dad (becoming like dad) by adopting his values. This makes the boy less threatening to dad and is the source of the boy's superego.

Girls, on the other hand, wake up one day and realize they're missing a penis, wish they had one (**penis envy**), and desire their father. Mom won't like that, but she also isn't very threatening (the girl has already been castrated!), so the girl isn't especially motivated to identify with her. As a result, girls have weaker superegos than boys do. This is a major source of criticism about psychoanalysis being sexist. Interestingly, though, it was Freud's daughter, Anna, who pushed the idea that girls go through this process.

Carl Roger

THE HUMANISTIC APPROACH

One other source of criticism about psychoanalysis is the idea that people are basically bad—sexually and aggressively impulsive and self-ish—and need to be restrained. According to the **humanistic approach** to personality, people are basically good and the world would be better off if they were allowed to express their true selves without restraints. Carl Rogers' **self theory** (or **person-centered theory**) is often used as an example of this approach. Rogers describes personality in terms of a **true self** (the talents, thoughts, desires, and feelings that we genuinely have), a **self-concept** (what we think we're like), and an **ideal self** (what we would like to be). You might think of these as the humanistic equivalents of id, ego, and superego, respectively. Similar to psychoanalysis, these parts of the personality can be in conflict (i.e., **incongruent**), and cause anxiety, which you can either protect yourself against with defense mechanisms or try to reconcile through **self-actualization** (accepting who you are as part of your self-concept and adjusting your ideals to reflect that; in other words, being all you can be). What throws people, especially children, off the path of self-actualization is **conditions of worth** imposed by parents and others. That is, parents can send the message to a child that he or she can only be valued by doing what the parents want. The child then has to deny his or her true self in order to please the parents. This situation can be avoided, or rectified, if the child is around others who are **empathic**, **accepting**, **genuine**, and who offer the child **unconditional positive regard**—an appreciation of who the child is, faults and all. As you might imagine, much of the immense literature on **self-esteem** has stemmed in one way or another from Rogers' theory.

THE SOCIAL-COGNITIVE APPROACH

A third way of explaining consistency in behavior in terms of personality focuses on **cognition** (how people think about themselves and their relations with the world around them) and is sometimes called the **social-cognitive approach**. One important contribution of this approach is the idea of **reciprocal determinism**: how people think, how people behave, and what their environment is like all interact to influence the consistency of behavior. For instance, if you're interested in tennis (a cognition), you'll consistently choose to play or watch tennis (behavior) and you'll be rewarded by being around people who share your enthusiasm for tennis (people who are part of the environment). These elements combined will strengthen your interest in tennis and thus maintain the consistency of your tennis-oriented behavior.

THE INDIVIDUAL-DIFFERENCE (OR TRAIT) APPROACH

There are many ways to slice up personality. People exhibit all sorts of traits, motives, and cognitions. The **individual-difference approach** to personality is not so much about "big" theories as it is about measuring the many, many ways in which people differ, reducing those many ways down to a more manageable subset, and using measurements of those characteristics to predict actual behavior.

Efforts along these lines have focused mainly on **traits**—consistent patterns of behavior. Traits are usually measured using **self-report questionnaires**, which typically ask people to judge their agreement with statements describing behavior that might be indicative of a particular trait. "I'm willing to help people who need it," for example, might be indicative of an "altruistic" trait. Someone trying to understand what personality is all about, however, might have a daunting time using traits to do it. After all, there are approximately 18,000 trait terms in the English language. The **Big Five** personality traits represent an attempt to reduce all those ways of describing people down to just a few fundamental dimensions of personality. The strategy behind this essentially involved measuring many traits and then using a statistical procedure called **factor analysis** to identify traits for which scores correlate highly with each other, presumably because they measure very much the same thing and are fundamental to describing what personality is all about. The result was the Big Five: **Openness** (inquiring, independent, curious), **Conscientiousness** (dependable, self-controlled), **Extraversion** (outgoing, socially adaptive), **Agreeableness** (conforming, likable), and **Neuroticism** (excitabilty, anxiousness).

CHAPTER 11

Psychological Disorders

Chapter 11

PSYCHOLOGICAL DISORDERS

The branch of psychology that deals with psychological disorders is called **abnormal psychology**. The classic way to define abnormality, or disorder, is in terms of patterns of thoughts, feelings, or behaviors that interfere with a person's ability to function at work, in relationships, or at leisure. Approximately 300 disorders are described in the *DSM-IV (The Diagnostic and Statistical Manual)*, of the American Psychiatric Association and are simply different patterns of abnormal behavior that have been grouped together into categories in order to make diagnosis simpler and more reliable than it otherwise would be. The disorders in any given category share some, but not all the characteristics of other disorders and are distinctly different from disorders in other categories.

ANXIETY DISORDERS

Anxiety disorders compose a class of disorders involving inexplicable or unusual feelings of dread, fearfulness, or terror as its defining feature. Individuals with **generalized anxiety disorder** feel persistent anxiety, but are unaware of its source (thus it's sometimes called "free-floating" anxiety). It may also be accompanied by physical symptoms including sweaty palms, shaking, or nervous habits like nail-biting. Rather than involving persistent fear, **panic disorder** involves unpredictable, minutes-long episodes of terror that have a sudden onset. These panic attacks are generally accompanied by a racing heart, breathlessness, dizziness, and other signs of intense fear. As discussed in previous chapters, **phobias** are characterized by intense and irrational fears of specific objects or events. **Obsessive-compulsive disorder** (or **OCD**) involves repetitive thoughts (obsessions) that provoke anxiety and repetitive behaviors (compulsions). Obsessions often include a preoccupation with germs and dirt, impending disaster, or neatness. Compulsions often include checking locks on doors, hygiene-related rituals such as hand washing or tooth brushing, and repeatedly checking that appliances or lights have been turned off when leaving home.

MOOD DISORDERS

Mood disorders are characterized by depression, mania, or both. A **major depressive disorder**, for example, is characterized by feelings of sadness, hopelessness, and discouragement (all lasting at least two weeks), and a loss of interest in pleasurable activities. **Bipolar disorders** involve swings back and forth between states of depression and states of heightened excitement and risk-taking optimism called **mania**.

DISSOCIATIVE DISORDERS

Dissociative disorders include as a feature the fragmentation of personality. That is, the individual behaves as if one part of his or her experience (consciousness, memories, identity) is separated from other parts (i.e., has "dissociated"). Thus, **dissociative amnesia** involves being unable to remember personally relevant information. Typically, the inability to recall this information is brought about by stressful events; therefore, the memory loss can't be attributed to ordinary forgetfulness. Someone in a **dissociative fugue** travels away from home or work suddenly and unexpectedly, can't recall his or her past, and becomes confused about his or her identity, sometimes assuming a new identity. **Dissociative identity disorder** is characterized by the expression of two or more distinctly different identities from the same person. The individual appears to be controlled by one of these identities at a time and typically has trouble remembering personal information associated with other identities. (This used to be called "multiple personality disorder.")

SCHIZOPHRENIA

Schizophrenia, which for some reason has often been confused with having multiple personalities, is a disorder involving symptoms of **psychosis** (i.e., hallucinations and delusions). **Hallucinations** are false sensations that include hearing voices that aren't there or seeing objects that don't exist. **Delusions** are false thoughts; for example, believing you're someone famous (Jesus, Teddy Roosevelt, and so forth). Thus schizophrenics have trouble distinguishing between the real world and their own fantasy or imagination. Additional symptoms might include incoherent speech, unusual behavior (the person may exhibit wild and disorganized thoughts or actions, or assume a completely motionless position), and dull, flat emotions.

   <u>**Types of Schizophrenia.**</u> Schizophrenia can be broken down into several types. **Paranoid schizophrenics** typically exhibit **delusions of grandeur** (believing themselves to be important, and usually famous people) or **delusions of persecution** (believing that they will be harmed by others) and often have auditory hallucinations that reinforce the theme of their delusions (e.g., hearing a voice tell them they're being watched). **Disorganized schizophrenics** have the other common symptoms of schizophrenia: disorganized speech or behavior, and inappropriate emotional responses. The key feature of **catatonic schizophrenia** is odd motor activity. Catatonics may be excessively active and agitated (without any obvious reason or purpose) or immobile. They sometimes also have a condition called **waxy flexibility** ("catalepsy"), in which they put their limbs in some position and leave them there for long periods of time. Other common catatonic symptoms are **echolalia**—senselessly repeating back words someone else has just said—and **echopraxia** (repeating other people's movements). Someone with **undifferentiated schizophrenia** can exhibit symptoms of any type of schizophrenia, but do not meet the specific criteria for having one of the other forms of schizophrenia.

SOMATOFORM DISORDERS

   The central feature of **somatoform disorders** is that the individual has physical symptoms usually associated with some sort of disease or physical disorder, but the symptoms can't be explained in terms of a medical condition. **Conversion disorders**, for example, involve impaired motor functioning (e.g., paralysis) or impaired sensory functioning (e.g., blindness) that can't be attributed to any neurological problems, but could be attributed to psychological factors (e.g., stress). Someone with **hypochondriasis** doesn't necessarily have any actual physical problems, but is nevertheless pre-occupied with bodily symptoms of disease or illness, is afraid he or she has a serious medical problem, and can't be reassured by medical doctors.

PERSONALITY DISORDERS

   Personality disorders are characterized by patterns of behavior or thinking (i.e., personality) that are clearly and substantially inconsistent with the expectations of one's culture. A **paranoid personality**, for example, is extremely suspicious and distrustful (but, unlike the paranoid schizophrenic personality, is not delusional). A person with an **antisocial personality** tramples on the rights of others, is impulsive, and lacks a conscience. Someone with a **borderline personality disorder** has trouble maintaining relationships and has wide fluctuations in both self-image and emotional behaviors. A **narcissistic personality** needs undue admiration and praise, is pre-occupied with fantasies of success, accomplishment, and recognition, feels entitled to special treatment, and lacks empathy for others.

EXPLANATIONS FOR ABNORMAL BEHAVIOR

In addition to describing patterns of maladaptive behavior (i.e., psychological disorders), psychologists also attempt to *explain* where that behavior came from. Broadly speaking, there are four basic approaches to explaining abnormality. The **medical approach** offers explanations that focus on physiological or biological reasons: the effects of drugs and alcohol, toxins (like lead or mercury), physical injury (e.g., head trauma), and genetics. For example, people become depressed because they have too much or too little of certain neurotransmitters. The **psychoanalytic approach** focuses on the possibility that unconscious conflicts, rooted in early childhood, cause anxiety that is then dealt with in a maladaptive way. If you're depressed, it's perhaps because you've directed anger you felt toward your mother toward yourself instead. The **cognitive approach** explains abnormal behavior in terms of abnormal patterns of thinking. People who are depressed tend to explain their success in terms of something outside themselves (like luck or other people's generosity) and their failures in terms of something inside themselves (such as stupidity or a lack of talent). According to the **learning** or **behavioral approach**, the problem behavior itself is the problem; that is, psychological disorders are not merely symptoms of some other underlying problem. From this perspective, disorders are learned behaviors; they've been either classically conditioned or reinforced in some way. If you're depressed, it's because you've been reinforced for staying in bed late, acting mopey, and withdrawing from other people. As discussed in the next chapter, each of these approaches to explaining abnormal behavior also suggests some possible treatments for it.

▼

CHAPTER 12

Psychological Therapies

Chapter 12

PSYCHOLOGICAL THERAPIES

The focus of any treatment for psychological disorders is changing a maladaptive pattern of behavior or thinking. Broadly speaking, there are **medical approaches**, which rely on drugs and surgery, and **psychological approaches**, which emphasize some sort of relationship between a client (the person with the disorder) and a therapist. Psychological approaches include psychoanalysis, humanistic therapies, behavior modification, and cognitive therapies.

THE PSYCHOANALYTIC APPROACH

Psychoanalysis was originally developed by Freud and his followers. Although it's an uncommon form of treatment today, a number of the therapeutic techniques, terms, and assumptions about abnormality that psychoanalysis describes are still commonly used. According to psychoanalytic thinking, problems arise when urges (primarily sexual ones) come up against social pressures to squelch them (from parents, mostly). These conflicts first take place in childhood, when children might not have enough "ego" to deal with them effectively, and in turn, gradually generate anxiety, which the child avoids by **repressing** the conflict (i.e., by keeping the conflict unconscious). The conflict may nevertheless be expressed through abnormal behavior. The goal of psychoanalytic therapies, then, is to help the individual recognize the conflict—make it conscious—and deal with it in a socially acceptable and productive way.

One method for making the conflict conscious is by **free association**. This involves having the individual relax as much as possible and say whatever comes to mind (often by starting with a recent emotional experience, dream, or memory). The objective is to provide conditions that will allow the person to gain access to memories of the original conflict so that he or she can achieve **insight** by using those formerly repressed memories to understand current behavior. And because dealing with those memories by repressing them took a lot of energy, lots of energy will become available for other, presumably healthier activities when the conflict is no longer being forced out of consciousness. This "liberation" of energy is called **catharsis**. Of course, people put up **resistance** to becoming aware of thoughts they've repressed by actively controlling what they say and do in order to avoid the anxiety-provoking thoughts. As examples, someone might resist by "forgetting" something threatening he or she was about to say or by suddenly claiming to be sick and leaving the therapy session. One clue a therapist might use to figure out what people are repressing is **transference**—expressions toward the therapist that indicate feelings linked to earlier relationships. Although people often resist becoming aware of these feelings, such as hatred toward their mother or father, the feelings may nevertheless leak out in behavior they direct toward the therapist.

THE HUMANISTIC APPROACH

Humanistic therapies are also geared toward helping people achieve insight into the causes of their problematic behavior, but the emphasis is more on what's happening in the client's life now and what the client wants for the future than it is on the client's childhood. (Carl Rogers, a humanist, preferred to use the term **client** to refer to someone in therapy, whereas psychoanalysts tend to use the term **patient**.) Also, **client-centered therapy** (Rogers' extremely influential version of a humanistic therapy) is non-directive; rather than offering interpretations of the client's behavior, client-centered therapists assume that people can achieve insight on their own if given the proper environment. As described in the chapter on personality, people's lives veer off course when others (such as parents) impose conditions of worth. In order to help the client recognize his or her true goals, then, it's up to the therapist to provide unconditional positive regard and an environment in which others (in this case, the therapist) are empathic, accepting, and genuine. Rogers introduced the technique of **active listening** as a way to accomplish this. This involves paraphrasing what the client says, asking for clarification and elaboration, and "reflecting" the client's feelings (i.e., stating what the client appears to feel: "It sounds as though that made you angry," for example).

THE COGNITIVE APPROACH

Cognitive therapies, too, assume that something going on inside the individual is responsible for abnormal behavior: People behave in abnormal ways because of the way they think. The difference between cognitive approaches and the ones discussed earlier in this chapter is that there isn't any assumption that conflict or anxiety is the cause of the problem behavior (although it might be a symptom of the problem). A cognitive therapist's aim, then, is to change the individual's thinking so that he or she sees the world accurately and rationally. This would then make it possible for the person to react to people and events in rational, productive ways and to direct his or her behavior toward healthy, fulfilling goals.

THE LEARNING (OR BEHAVIORAL) APPROACH

Behavioral therapies—referred to collectively as **behavior modification**—aren't aimed at achieving insight or self-awareness, or even a change in thinking. They rely instead on using principles of classical and operant conditioning to change problem behaviors directly. From this perspective, abnormal behaviors were either conditioned to begin with (throwing temper tantrums, for example) and therefore can be "un"-conditioned; or they weren't originally conditioned (e.g., bedwetting) but can nevertheless be eliminated through operant or classical conditioning.

Recall that classical conditioning involves the pairing of a neutral stimulus with another stimulus (the unconditioned stimulus, or US) that elicits some automatic response (the unconditioned response, or UR). As the result of that pairing, the neutral stimulus becomes a conditioned stimulus, or CS, that (typically) produces the same response the US did (the conditioned response, or CR). Problem behaviors can often be thought of as conditioned responses. This is the case with phobias: A person learns to be afraid of strangers (a CS), for instance, because interactions with strangers have been paired in some way with something inherently unpleasant (a US, such as ridicule or teasing). If the behavior has been learned, how can it be eliminated?

Counterconditioning involves conditioning a new response that's incompatible with an old response. In a procedure called **systematic desensitization**, anxiety is gradually replaced with relaxation. The process starts by exposing the client to a mild form of the fear-arousing situation, often simply imagining it, and then having him or her relax (relaxation techniques can be taught prior to starting a systematic desensitization program). Next, a situation somewhat more like the fear-arousing one is imagined, followed by relaxation. Then another, and so on, each situation becoming progressively more like the one that arouses the most fear. Eventually, the client enters real situations that approximate the fear-arousing situation, relaxing each time, until he or she can confront the phobic object (the CS) itself and feel relaxed. For example, he or she might think about seeing strangers outside, relax, then think about saying hello to a stranger, relax, then think about having a conversation with a stranger, and so on until an actual stranger is confronted. In a variant of this called **flooding**, the person goes straight into the fear-provoking situation without the intermediate steps. Assuming strangers don't actually do anything hurtful (which would generally be arranged in advance by the therapist), the CR would simply be extinguished.

In **aversive conditioning**, an unpleasant response becomes associated with what would normally be a pleasant activity. To treat alcoholism, for example, an alcoholic drink (the CS) might be paired with a drug (the US) that makes the drinker nauseous (the UR and CR). The drinker should then become nauseous when anticipating drinking and, therefore, avoid alcohol.

Several other types of therapies are based on principles of operant conditioning, usually focusing on rewarding desirable behaviors and eliminating rewards for undesirable ones (punishing undesirable behaviors can often create more problems than it solves). In a **token economy**, the individual is given some sort of token (such as a poker chip, or even simply a gold star next to his or her name on a piece of paper) whenever the desired behavior is performed. When the individual has accumulated enough of them, the tokens can then be "cashed in" for tangible rewards (food, the opportunity to play a game, a trip to the zoo, and so forth).

THE BIOLOGICAL (OR MEDICAL) APPROACH

Biological or **medical therapies**, which rely on drugs or surgery, alter the way the brain functions. Depression, for example, is accompanied by low levels of the neurotransmitter serotonin at synapses in the brain. **Anti-depressant drugs**, like Prozac, Paxil, and Zoloft, prevent the re-uptake of serotonin (they're SSRIs: selective serotonin re-uptake inhibitors) and eventually result in an elevated mood. **Anti-anxiety drugs** (such as Librium or Valium) reduce arousal by depressing activity in the central nervous system. **Anti-psychotics** (like Clozapine or Thorazine) that treat the symptoms of schizophrenia block the operation of the neurotransmitter dopamine, which is overabundant in people with psychotic symptoms.

CHAPTER 13

Social
Psychology

Chapter 13

SOCIAL PSYCHOLOGY

Social psychology has to do with how the behavior of individuals is influenced by other people. The field of social psychology is commonly broken into three areas: social cognition, social influence, and social relationships.

SOCIAL COGNITION

Social cognition refers to how we process information about other people. **Attribution theory**, for example, deals with the types of explanations people generate for others' behavior and how those explanations come about. Broadly speaking, there are two types of attributions (explanations for behavior) that a person could come up with: **dispositional** (or **internal**) **attributions** explain behavior in terms of factors inside the person (personality, intelligence, maturity, and so forth), whereas **situational** (or **external**) **attributions** explain behavior in terms of factors outside the person (such as luck, interference from other people, social etiquette, etc.). These attributions then presumably influence our behavior: If someone has complimented you on your new hair style and you attribute it to his or her ability to appreciate your good taste (a dispositional attribution), then you might respond warmly to this person; if you attribute the compliment to pressure from his or her boss to sell you a life insurance policy (an external attribution), then you might walk away.

Originally, attribution theorists thought of the attribution process as rational and logical. It isn't. One prominent bias in how people explain behavior is called the **actor-observer difference:** Observers tend to attribute others' behavior to dispositions (this is called the **fundamental attribution error**), but their own behavior (as the actor) to situations. This is due, at least in part, to the actor being more aware than others are of how his or her behavior changes from one situation to another.

A second way in which attributions can be less than rational is often described in terms of **cognitive dissonance theory**. According to this theory, if you behave in a way that's inconsistent with one of your attitudes, the inconsistency will produce **dissonance**, an unpleasant state of tension. You can't undo your behavior, so to eliminate the dissonance, you feel compelled to explain what you did in a way that will allow you to feel comfortable again. One of those ways would be to explain your behavior in terms of something situational (e.g., "I was paid so much money I couldn't have not done it!"). Another way would be to explain your behavior in terms of something internal. But it can't be your current attitude, because that's inconsistent with your behavior. The solution? Change your attitude (e.g., "I guess I like doing that more than I thought.").

SOCIAL INFLUENCE

Our own behavior can influence our attitudes (and, so, our future behavior), but so of course can other people. **Social influence** is about the direct and indirect pressures exerted by others to change someone's attitudes or behavior. Some of these pressures come in the form of deliberate strategies. The **foot-in-the-door technique**, for example, involves getting someone to comply with a small request before asking him or her to comply with a larger request; "May I borrow a cup of sugar? Thanks. Now may I borrow your car?" After complying with the smaller request, people are more likely to comply with the larger request than they otherwise would be. The **door-in-the-face technique** works in the other direction: making a request that's so big it'll be turned down before making a smaller, more reasonable request; "May I borrow your car? No? How about five bucks for a cab?" **Lowballing** involves getting someone to commit to doing something, then increasing the effort or cost required to fulfill the commitment; "Will you do me a favor? Yes? Can I borrow your car?"

Other forms of influence simply happen because other people are around. **Conformity** has to do with changing behavior in order to make it consistent with group norms. In a famous experiment, **Solomon Asch** asked participants to judge which of three lines on a piece of paper was the same length as a fourth line. Unbeknownst to the actual research subjects, the other participants were working for Asch (i.e., they were confederates) and had been instructed to give the same wrong answer. Over a series of these judgment trials, subjects conformed to the confederates' (very obviously) wrong answers about two-thirds of the time.

Behavior in the Asch study is an example of **normative social influence**: Pressure to comply with a norm (even one that's obviously wrong) comes from concern about being rejected by the group (when asked why they conformed, many of Asch's subjects said essentially that). But in ambiguous situations, in which there are no norms to conform to and no clear bases for deciding how to behave, people often react to **informational social influence**. In other words, what other people do simply provides information about how to behave. If you're not sure whether an acquaintance has made a joke, for example, you might wait to see whether other people laugh before you laugh.

The most direct form of social influence would be **obedience**: doing what an authority figure tells you to do. Another famous social psychology experiment, this one by **Stanley Milgram**, demonstrated that people can be incredibly susceptible to the demands of an authority. As part of a phony learning study, Milgram convinced subjects that they would be delivering progressively stronger shocks—up to 450 volts, marked on a panel in front of the subject as "XXX, Danger! Severe shock!"— to someone for giving wrong answers to questions the subjects would be asking (no shocks were actually delivered). As the shocks supposedly got stronger, the "learner" became more and more distressed (eventually complaining of chest pains and refusing to answer more questions). The "teachers" typically objected to continuing with the shocks, but the experimenter (looking and sounding authoritative) insisted that the teachers continue. Although a group of psychiatrists had estimated that fewer than one percent of subjects would be sadistic enough to continue with shocks until the end (i.e., 450 volts), 63% of subjects in Milgram's initial study actually did just that. Later studies, though, showed that obedience was less likely when 1) the authority figure wasn't close by, 2) the victim/learner was visible, and 3) other subjects disobeyed the experimenter.

SOCIAL RELATIONS — AGGRESSION AND ALTRUISM

Much of the research on social relationships has to do with aggression and altruism. **Aggression** involves behaviors that are intended to hurt others. According to the **frustration-aggression hypothesis**, aggression is always the product of frustration and frustration always leads to aggression. This analysis was clearly wrong (e.g., frustration sometimes just leads to crying), but did generate research showing that any aversive event (e.g., hot temperatures, smelly rooms, crowds) can produce aggression, depending on a variety of factors. **Testosterone**, a hormone that is normally at much higher levels in men than in women, appears to lower thresholds for aggression: People, and animals, with higher levels of test-osterone are more easily provoked to aggression. The presence of **aggressive cues** (such as guns, knives, black clothing, or aggressive behavior by others) also leads to higher levels of aggression among people who have already been provoked (in experiments, this is often accomplished by having a confederate of the experimenter insult the subject). This phenomenon is called the **weapons effect.** Aggression can also be learned: Children who see aggression being modeled on television, for instance, are more likely to become aggressive if they see the aggression rewarded (and are less likely to become aggressive if they see it being punished).

Altruism, on the other hand, is behavior aimed at unselfishly helping others (practically, though, the distinction between unselfish helping and selfish helping is often hard to make convincingly). Research into helping behavior was catalyzed by the murder of **Kitty Genovese**, a young woman who was raped and murdered in her New York City neighborhood in 1964, despite the fact that there were 38 witnesses to the act (none of whom called the police until after the murderer fled). Although people were shocked at the witnesses' behavior, it turns out that, in an emergency, increasing the number of witnesses (i.e., bystanders) decreases the likelihood that any of them will help. This diffusion of responsibility leads to the **bystander effect**.

Yet people often do help. Why? According to **social-exchange theory**, our goal in life is to maximize our rewards and minimize our costs (the **minimax principle**), so if helping someone will benefit us more than it will hurt us, we'll help. Another explanation has to do with normative social influence, discussed earlier. There appear to be two norms that would encourage helping behavior: The **social responsibility norm** is that we're obligated to help people who need our help; the **reciprocity norm** is that we're obligated to help those who have helped us. A third explanation is that helping behavior has evolved. One version of this explanation is called the **kin selection hypothesis**. The idea is that those of our ancestors who were genetically predisposed to help their relatives (their kin) would also have been helping to pass on their own genes (because their relatives shared their genes). Over time, then, their genes (including the ones that predispose helping kin) would have spread throughout the human species. Thus we wouldn't help indiscriminately, we'd be biased toward helping those who are like us and, so, who are likely to share our genes. In fact, people are generally more likely to help close relatives than distant ones, and distant relatives more than strangers.

CHAPTER 14

Testing, Measurement, and Statistics

Chapter 14

TESTING, MEASUREMENT, AND STATISTICS

In order to treat mental disorders, study behavior, and assess mental functioning, psychologists (and others) have come up with a wide variety of psychological tests. These tests measure things like personality, intelligence, and aptitudes for various activities and generally produce a score that describes how much of some psychological characteristic (like intelligence) a person has in comparison to others who took the test. Developing these tests, and using them in research, isn't as easy or straightforward as it might seem.

RELIABILITY, VALIDITY, AND STANDARDIZATION

Any measure of a psychological characteristic must be reliable and valid. **Reliability** refers to the consistency of people's scores on a test. This can be assessed in a number of ways. **Test-retest reliability** refers to the consistency of scores across administrations of the test. If taking the test on more than one occasion, do people get about the same score the second time that they did the first time? When an adequate number of people have taken the test twice, the researcher developing the test can compute a correlation coefficient between the two sets of scores (are scores from the first administration correlated highly with scores from the second administration?). Coefficients larger than about +.70 are generally considered adequate evidence of reliability (although that varies depending on the type of test, what it's measuring, and what the scores are being used for). The reliability of self-report measures is typically described in terms of **internal consistency**: How well does the test correlate with itself? This is often assessed as **split-half reliability**. For each test-taker, a score is generated for, say, all the even-numbered test items (perhaps by simply totaling up ratings for those items), as well as for the odd-numbered items, and a correlation coefficient is computed across the two sets of scores. Thanks to math, and computers, the split-half reliability of a test can actually be calculated as the average correlation for every possible way of splitting the test in half. This measure of reliability is called **Cronbach's alpha**.

Validity refers to how well a test measures what it's supposed to measure. If the reliability of a psychological test is low, it can't possibly measure what it's supposed to measure—some enduring, stable psychological characteristic. Thus it can't be valid if it isn't reliable. But being reliable is no guarantee that the test is valid; it could be measuring the same wrong thing over and over. For example, if a personality test had people rate how much they gossip, it's possible that individuals would get the same score every time they took the test (which would indicate reliability), but these scores could merely reflect how concerned they are about coming across well on a personality test. This test would therefore have a low validity.

There are several ways to assess validity. **Face validity** (or **content validity**) refers simply to whether the test looks as though it's measuring what it's supposed to. This is fine for, say, a driver's test, but not adequate for most psychological tests. **Predictive validity** refers to how well scores on the test predict actual behavior of the type the test is supposed to measure. **Construct validity** refers to whether scores on the questionnaire are related in expected ways (i.e., positively or negatively) to scores on other questionnaires.

Often, tests have been **standardized**—given to a large number of people with some known characteristics (such as age, sex, or race)—in order to make it possible to determine how well a person has performed relative to others who have taken the test. Knowing how many problems you've gotten right on an intelligence test, for instance, is meaningless without knowing how well other people of your age have done.

DESCRIPTIVE STATISTICS AND STATISTICAL INFERENCE

When conducting an experiment or correlational study (the most common types of psychological research), the researcher virtually always measures behavior in a **sample** (a representative subset) of people drawn from some larger **population** (such as all Americans, all college students, all female high-school students with an eating disorder, etc.). That sample's scores on your measures can be described precisely using several **descriptive statistics**. The **mode** is the most commonly occurring score; the **median** is the score above which half of all scores fall; and the **mean** is the arithmetic average of all scores (add all the scores up and divide by the number of scores that have been added). One could also determine the **standard deviation**, an index of how widely scattered scores tend to be around the mean.

But people who are interested in a researcher's findings are rarely interested in what the researcher's sample is like. They're interested in what the population from which the sample came is like. It's all well and good that, in my sample, a measure of self-esteem was correlated with a measure of how often people initiate conversations, but is that true for people in general?

Inferential statistics allow you to make inferences about populations based on the characteristics of your sample. To do this, researchers use tests of **statistical significance**. To understand statistical significance, keep in mind that any relationship (in a correlational study) or any difference between two means (in an experiment) could have happened by chance. There will never be any way to know. If a relationship or a difference is statistically significant, it simply means that it wasn't likely to have happened by chance if there weren't a relationship (or difference) in the population your samples came from.

In other words, if two variables are uncorrelated in a population of people and you draw a sample of those people for your study, those variables might still be correlated (to one extent or another) in your sample—just by chance. If it's just by chance, though, the correlation coefficient in your sample should be somewhere near .00; after all, that's the true correlation in your population. The bigger the coefficient is in your sample, then, the more confident you can be that the true correlation isn't .00.

There's a way to estimate how likely you would have been to get the coefficient you got if: 1) you had repeated your study an infinite number of times and 2) there wasn't really a relationship between the two variables in the population your sample came from. By consensus, a coefficient that would only show up 5% of the time or less, when the true population correlation is zero, is statistically significant. In an experiment, a statistically significant difference is one that would show up 5% of the time or less if there really were no difference between the populations from which your two samples were selected.

PRACTICE TEST 1

This test is also on CD-ROM in our special interactive CLEP Introductory Psychology TEST*ware*®. It is highly recommended that you first take this exam on computer. You will then have the additional study features and benefits of enforced timed conditions, individual diagnostic analysis, and instant scoring. See page ix for guidance on how to get the most out of our CLEP Introductory Psychology software.

CLEP INTRODUCTORY PSYCHOLOGY

Practice Test 1

(Answer sheets appear in the back of this book.)

TIME: 90 Minutes
100 Questions

DIRECTIONS: Each of the questions or incomplete statements below is followed by five possible answers or completions. Select the best choice in each case and fill in the corresponding oval on the answer sheet.

---

1. Which of the following is the philosophical approach to studying human behavior that emphasizes the purpose or usefulness of behavior?

   (A) Structuralism   (D) Psychoanalysis

   (B) Behaviorism   (E) Humanism

   (C) Functionalism

2. Which of the following approaches is used by a psychologist who studies depression by examining levels of a certain neurotransmitter in the brains of depressed and non-depressed people?

   (A) psychoanalytic   (D) cognitive

   (B) behavioral   (E) biological

   (C) humanistic

3. Which of the following approaches is used by a psychologist who emphasizes the power of rewards and punishments to influence behavior?

    (A) behavioral   (D) psychoanalytic

    (B) cognitive   (E) biological

    (C) humanistic

4. A researcher wants to know whether failure at a task causes aggression. As part of her study, some subjects are told they have failed at a task, whereas others are told they have succeeded. Failing or not at the task would be

    (A) a placebo.

    (B) the independent variable.

    (C) a within-subjects manipulation.

    (D) the dependent variable.

    (E) a counterbalancing procedure.

5. A researcher sits at a table in a restaurant all day and records what customers in adjoining booths are saying and doing. What type of research strategy is this?

    (A) Experiment   (D) Survey

    (B) Correlational study   (E) Naturalistic observation

    (C) Case study

6. Which of the following correlation coefficients represents the strongest relationship between two variables?

    (A) +.31   (D) −.81

    (B) −.06   (E) +.50

    (C) +.73

7. Random assignment of subjects to experimental and control groups ensures that

    (A) the number of subjects in each group will be the same.

    (B) subjects in each condition will not know each other.

(C) prior to the experimental manipulation, the two groups of subjects would be equivalent with respect to the dependent variable.

(D) prior to the experimental manipulation, the two groups of subjects would be equivalent with respect to the independent variable.

(E) after the experimental manipulation, the two groups of subjects would differ with respect to the dependent variable.

8. "Nature" is to "nurture" as _____ is to _____.

(A) genetics; environment

(D) upbringing; social status

(B) biology; physiology

(E) social status; biology

(C) physiology; genetics

9. Which of the following areas of the brain, located at the top of the spinal cord, regulates breathing, waking, and heartbeat?

(A) Thalamus

(D) Medulla

(B) Reticular formation

(E) Cerebellum

(C) Parietal lobe

10. The simplest cell of the nervous system is a

(A) neuron

(D) soma

(B) dendrite

(E) terminal buttons

(C) axon

11. Which of the following greatly speeds up the transmission of signals through a neuron?

(A) Dendrites

(D) An action potential

(B) A myelin sheath

(E) Vesicles

(C) Depolarization

12. The period during which the neuron cannot fire is described as which of the following?

(A) Lock-up

(B) Absolute refractory period

(C) Resting period

(D) Reset period

(E) Hyper-polarization period

13. The Somatic Nervous System is part of the

(A) central nervous system

(B) peripheral nervous system

(C) autonomic nervous system

(D) sympathetic division

(E) parasympathetic division

14. The site in the auditory cortex located where acoustical codes are decoded and interpreted is known as

(A) Wernicke's area

(B) motor area

(C) visual association areas

(D) Broca's area

(E) pons

15. Which chemicals are responsible for the "runner's high" and important for controlling pleasure/pain properties?

(A) Adrenalines

(B) Steroids

(C) Acetylcholine

(D) Endorphins

(E) GABA

16. Neurons stimulate nearby glands, muscles, or other neurons through chemicals released from their

(A) axons

(B) somas

(C) dendrites

(D) terminal buttons

(E) nucleus

17. The reticular formation

(A) regulates heartbeat and breathing

(B) controls hunger

(C) helps control arousal

(D) regulates fear and aggression

(E) coordinates voluntary movement

18. The nervous system's ability to detect and encode energy from stimuli is called

(A) perception

(B) parallel processing

(C) top-down processing

(D) sensation

(E) subliminal perception

19. The minimum stimulation needed to detect a stimulus half of the time it's presented is called

(A) perception

(B) the absolute threshold

(C) the just-noticeable difference

(D) the difference threshold

(E) feature detection

20. Tina has a box of CDs that's twice as heavy as Gary's. Tina's box would have to have eight more CDs in it before it would feel heavier, whereas Gary's would have to have only four more CDs in it in order for it to feel heavier. This illustrates

(A) sensory adaptation

(B) Weber's Law

(C) the Young-Helmholtz theory

(D) opponent-process theory

(E) feature detection theory

21. By which process is stimulus energy converted into neural messages?

(A) Transduction

(B) Feature detection

(C) Perceptual set

(D) Parallel processing

(E) Accommodation

22. Which type of cell allows us to distinguish different wavelengths of light?

    (A) Ganglion cells   (D) Rods

    (B) Cones   (E) Auditory

    (C) Bipolar cells

23. Which of the following is a binocular cue for perceiving distance?

    (A) Interposition   (D) Relative clarity

    (B) Motion parallax   (E) Convergence

    (C) Linear perspective

24. The fact that parallel lines appear to converge as they get farther away is referred to as

    (A) retinal disparity   (D) interposition

    (B) relative motion   (E) linear perspective

    (C) a texture gradient

25. When a series of lights on a movie marquee are turned on and off, one after the other, in succession, it appears that a single light is moving around the marquee. This illustrates

    (A) shape constancy   (D) perceptual set

    (B) linear perspective   (E) the phi phenomenon

    (C) perceptual adaptation

26. A circadian rhythm is

    (A) the body's reaction to changes in phases of the moon

    (B) the shifting from one stage of sleep to another

    (C) a hypnotic state

    (D) any pattern of biological functioning that happens over (roughly) a 24-hour cycle

    (E) changes in moods during a 28-day period of time

27. If someone is awake, has his or her eyes closed, and is in a relaxed state, an EEG would most likely indicate the presence of

    (A) alpha waves
    (B) sleep spindles
    (C) delta waves
    (D) rapid eye movements
    (E) large, slow brain waves

28. During which stage of sleep are hynogogic sensations most likely to occur?

    (A) Stage 1
    (B) Stage 2
    (C) Stage 3
    (D) Stage 4
    (E) REM

29. Among humans, the sleep cycle repeats itself every

    (A) hour
    (B) 90 minutes
    (C) 2 hours
    (D) 30 minutes
    (E) 45 minutes

30. Narcolepsy is a sleep disorder involving

    (A) difficulty waking up after a normal night of sleep
    (B) interruptions in breathing during sleep
    (C) having trouble staying asleep
    (D) having trouble falling asleep
    (E) uncontrollable attacks of intense sleepiness

31. The idea that the behavior of people who are hypnotized is controlled by normal, conscious processes is part of the theory that says hypnosis entails

    (A) REM rebound
    (B) hallucinations
    (C) role playing
    (D) dissociation
    (E) paradoxical sleep

32. Which of the following is involved in classical conditioning and operant conditioning, respectively?

(A) stimulus-stimulus pairings .. non-associative learning

(B) non-associative learning .. stimulus-response pairings

(C) stimulus-response pairings .. stimulus-stimulus pairings

(D) stimulus-stimulus pairings .. stimulus-response pairings

(E) associative learning .. non-associative learning

Questions 33 through 36 all refer to the following scenario: Wally is allergic to cat fur and it makes him sneeze violently. Anita has a lot of cats and her clothes often have cat fur on them. After three dates with Anita, Wally has begun to sneeze violently as soon as he sees her.

33. What type of learning does this illustrate?

   (A) Operant conditioning   (D) Classical conditioning

   (B) Vicarious learning   (E) Spontaneous recovery

   (C) Observational learning

34. In this example, cat fur would be a(n)

   (A) unconditioned stimulus   (D) model

   (B) reinforcer   (E) punisher

   (C) conditioned stimulus

35. In this example, sneezing would be

   (A) an unconditioned response, but not a conditioned response

   (B) a conditioned response, but not an unconditioned response

   (C) a punisher

   (D) a reinforcer

   (E) both an unconditioned response and a conditioned response

36. If, after the learning took place, Anita began to show up at Wally's without cat fur on her clothes, Wally's learned response would

   (A) extinguish   (D) be shaped

   (B) spontaneously recover   (E) discriminate

   (C) generalize

37. Bob gets a dollar for every magazine subscription he sells. What type of operant-conditioning consequence is maintaining Bob's selling?

    (A) Positive reinforcement   (D) Response-cost training

    (B) Negative reinforcement   (E) Partial reinforcement

    (C) Punishment

38. Lori has a glass of wine when she comes home every night because it relieves her unpleasant feelings of stress. Which operant-conditioning technique is maintaining Lori's drinking?

    (A) Positive reinforcement   (D) Response-cost training

    (B) Negative reinforcement   (E) Discrimination training

    (C) Punishment

39. Jeff won money in the state lottery after buying five tickets, then after buying six more tickets, then four more tickets (that is, after every fifth ticket, on average). Which reinforcement schedule maintains Jeff's ticket-buying behavior?

    (A) Continuous   (D) Fixed interval

    (B) Fixed ratio   (E) Variable interval

    (C) Variable ratio

40. Lucy whines when she doesn't get her way. Last Monday, her mother refused to give in to her whining for five minutes before finally giving Lucy what she was demanding. On Tuesday, her mother resisted for 10 minutes before giving in. On Wednesday, she resisted for 20 minutes. Lucy is being taught to whine for longer and longer periods of time through

    (A) discrimination training   (D) modeling

    (B) shaping   (E) punishment

    (C) partial reinforcement

41. Sally stopped hitting her brother when she saw a girl on a television show hit someone and then get in trouble for it. What type of learning on Sally's part does this illustrate?

(A) Latent learning   (D) Generalization

(B) Partial reinforcement   (E) Vicarious learning

(C) Shaping

42. A rule-of-thumb strategy for solving problems is called a(n)

(A) algorithm   (D) insight

(B) heuristic   (E) fixation

(C) prototype

43. After meeting Dave at a party, you decide he is shy. At several subsequent meetings, though, Dave is very outgoing. The idea that you're likely to continue believing Dave to be shy is called

(A) the framing effect

(B) belief perseverance

(C) overconfidence

(D) the availability heuristic

(E) the representativeness heuristic

44. A child saying "doll" while holding her hand out, as if expecting to be given the doll, would be an example of

(A) babbling   (D) telegraphic speech

(B) syntax   (E) echoic speech

(C) phonetics

45. A child's ability to recognize speech sounds that aren't used in its language begins to disappear during which stage of language development?

(A) The one-word stage   (D) The multi-word stage

(B) The babbling stage   (E) The telegraphic stage

(C) The two-word stage

46. Which of the following strategies should work best when studying for a test that's two weeks away?

(A) Don't begin studying until just a few hours before the test

(B) Do lots of studying during the first week, then relax during the second week

(C) Relax during the first week, then study intensely every day during the second week

(D) Study for an hour every day for two weeks

(E) Study once at the beginning of the two-week period

47. Remembering how to get from your house to a friend's house, without consciously knowing how to do it, is an example of

(A) iconic memory
(D) flashbulb memory

(B) implicit memory
(E) working memory

(C) echoic memory

48. Lori is 10 years old and has done as well on an intelligence test as the average 8-year-old. As originally calculated for the Stanford-Binet, what would Lori's IQ be?

(A) 100
(D) 8

(B) 125
(E) 80

(C) 10

49. Achievement tests

(A) how well someone is likely to do at a specific task

(B) measure the ability to learn

(C) measure learned skills or knowledge

(D) assess differences across people in the personality traits they have

(E) measure intelligence

50. Fixed and unlearned patterns of behavior that are characteristic of an entire species are called

(A) instincts
(D) extrinsic motives

(B) drives
(E) emotions

(C) incentives

51. A need is

    (A) an urge to do something in order to avoid punishment

    (B) an urge to do something in order to be rewarded

    (C) another term for "incentive"

    (D) a physiological condition that triggers motivation

    (E) a state of arousal

52. All of the following are considered "Big Five" personality traits EXCEPT

    (A) neuroticism

    (B) agreeableness

    (C) cathexis

    (D) extraversion

    (E) conscientiousness

53. The refractory period of the sexual response cycle

    (A) occurs just prior to orgasm

    (B) is the time period following a male's orgasm during which he can't be aroused to another orgasm

    (C) occurs immediately preceding ovulation

    (D) occurs immediately after ovulation

    (E) is the time during which sexual arousal is highest

54. According to the James-Lange theory of emotion,

    (A) emotional behavior is always learned, not innate

    (B) the experience of emotion causes physiological arousal

    (C) arousal and the subjective experience of emotion are triggered simultaneously by an emotion-arousing stimulus

    (D) one must label one's arousal in order to have an emotional experience

    (E) one must be aware of one's physiological arousal in order to experience emotion

55. After having three cups of strong coffee, you find that you're more angry than usual after being cut off in traffic, but you're also more scared than you would otherwise be when you hear someone walking behind you. Which theory of emotion explains why?

    (A) Two-factor theory   (D) Cannon-Bard

    (B) Instinct theory   (E) James-Lange

    (C) Opponent-process theory

56. As a general rule, performance at a task is best when arousal is

    (A) high   (D) worst

    (B) low   (E) non-existent

    (C) moderate

57. Charlie felt good about getting a C on his physics test until he found out that the average grade was a B. This change in the intensity of Charlie's happiness illustrates

    (A) the James-Lange theory

    (B) opponent-process theory

    (C) two-factor theory

    (D) the relative-deprivation principle

    (E) the adaptation-level phenomenon

58. Which of the following sequences of prenatal developmental stages is correct?

    (A) Embryo, fetus, zygote   (D) Fetus, zygote, embryo

    (B) Embryo, zygote, fetus   (E) Zygote, fetus, embryo

    (C) Zygote, embryo, fetus

59. Age being confounded with cohort will necessarily be a problem for which type of study?

    (A) Experiments   (D) Cross-sequential

    (B) Longitudinal   (E) Correlational

    (C) Cross-sectional

60. Three-year-old Tim, who sees lots of horses on his family's farm, saw a zebra at the zoo and thought it was a horse. Which of the cognitive processes described by Piaget does this illustrate?

    (A) Assimilation   (D) Egocentrism

    (B) Accommodation   (E) Object permanence

    (C) Conservation

61. After Samantha's father squashes the trash in the garbage can so that it takes up less space, Samantha thinks he's made the trash disappear. According to Piaget, why does she think so?

    (A) She hasn't assimilated the change in mass.

    (B) She's egocentric.

    (C) She accommodated the change in mass.

    (D) She isn't yet able to conserve mass.

    (E) She hasn't yet developed the capacity for formal operational thought.

62. The emotional bond that infants feel toward caregivers is called

    (A) accommodation   (D) sensitization

    (B) attachment   (E) an operation

    (C) imprinting

63. According to Erikson, the primary task of adolescence is to

    (A) learn to trust   (D) become competent

    (B) develop autonomy (E) develop an identity

    (C) acquire initiative

64. A cashier gave Ken $10 too much in change, but Ken gave it back because he was afraid he might get caught and punished if he tried to keep it. Ken is in which of Kohlberg's moral stages?

    (A) Concrete operational (D) Conventional

    (B) Formal operational   (E) Pre-conventional

    (C) Post-conventional

65. When given a list of words to remember, older adults

    (A) recognize and recall just as many as younger adults

    (B) recall fewer, but recognize as many as younger adults

    (C) recall more, but recognize fewer than younger adults

    (D) recognize more and recall more than younger adults

    (E) recognize fewer and recall fewer than younger adults

66. The knowledge and verbal skills that one has acquired over one's life are referred to as

    (A) crystallized intelligence

    (B) formal operational thought

    (C) fluid intelligence

    (D) concrete operational thought

    (E) conventional reasoning

67. According to psychoanalytic theory, the part of your personality that steers you toward socially acceptable behavior, even if it doesn't satisfy any needs, is called

    (A) the reality principle   (D) ego

    (B) id   (E) the self-concept

    (C) superego

68. Homer loves his wife deeply, but he also can't stand the fact that she leaves their car dirty whenever she drives it and he wants to tell her about his anger. According to the psychoanalytic theory, which part of Homer's personality can help him resolve the conflict between loving his wife and being angry at her?

    (A) Id   (D) The morality principle

    (B) Ego   (E) The ideal self

    (C) Superego

69. If Darlene plays basketball as a way to vent her angry impulses in a socially acceptable way, which defense mechanism is she using?

(A) Regression   (D) Reaction formation

(B) Rationalization   (E) Sublimation

(C) Projection

70. Relatively unique patterns of behavior are

(A) traits   (D) attitudes

(B) defense mechanisms   (E) reaction formations

(C) self-serving biases

71. From Carl Rogers' humanistic perspective, the most important aspect of personality is

(A) id

(B) the conscience

(C) the collective unconscious

(D) the self

(E) superego

72. Laura is an outgoing woman, so she goes to lots of social events. Being at social events, she's encouraged by others to be outgoing. This pattern of expressing a trait and then having its expression reinforced by others, illustrates

(A) the Barnum effect

(B) locus of control

(C) unconditional positive regard

(D) the self-serving bias

(E) reciprocal determinism

73. Multiple-personality is a rare form of which category of psychological disorders?

(A) Anxiety   (D) Schizophrenia

(B) Dissociative   (E) Personality

(C) Hypochondriasis

74. Wally is 30 years old and lives at home with his parents. He frequently takes money out of his mother's purse, has killed the neighbor's cat for coming into his yard, and shoots at passing cars with a BB gun. He doesn't feel badly about any of this. Which personality disorder does Wally have?

    (A) Antisocial

    (B) Narcissistic

    (C) Schizophrenia

    (D) Dissociative

    (E) Obsessive-compulsive

75. Larry often feels nervous and anxious, but he doesn't know why. Occasionally, his heart will start pounding for no apparent reason and he'll break out in a cold sweat. Which disorder does Larry have?

    (A) Bipolar

    (B) Phobia

    (C) Generalized anxiety

    (D) Dissociative identity

    (E) Conversion

76. Lucy washes her hands every time she touches anything someone else has touched. She also runs dishes through the dishwasher several times in succession before putting them away. Which psychological disorder does Lucy have?

    (A) Catatonic schizophrenia

    (B) Obsessive-compulsive

    (C) Antisocial personality

    (D) Schizophrenia

    (E) Somatoform

77. Archie has been working at a car wash in Chicago for a month. He has a number of documents that say his real name is Luther Hunt and that he lives in Pittsburgh, has a wife and two kids, and has a job as a stockbroker. Archie remembers none of this. Which disorder does Archie have?

    (A) Narcissistic personality

    (B) Bipolar

    (C) Anti-social personality

    (D) Schizophrenia

    (E) Dissociative fugue

78. Dave's mother occasionally has outbursts of uncontrollable behavior, but usually sits motionless in a chair. Dave once tried to help his mother feed herself by lifting her hand up to her mouth, but when he let go her hand remained in mid-air. Which form of schizophrenia does Dave's mother have?

    (A) Paranoid   (D) Catatonic

    (B) Residual   (E) Undifferentiated

    (C) Disorganized

79. Allison's parents fight constantly. They're loud and violent, and Allison hates it. One day she woke up to find that she could no longer hear. Which disorder does Allison have?

    (A) Conversion   (D) Panic

    (B) Schizophrenia   (E) Dissociative identity

    (C) Mood

80. Having a patient relax as much as possible and say whatever comes into his or her mind is central to the technique of

    (A) systematic desensitization

    (B) a token economy

    (C) free association

    (D) rational-emotive therapy

    (E) counter-conditioning

81. Tina wants desperately for her therapist to tell her that he'll take care of her and make sure she's always alright. These are things she wanted from her father, too, but was never able to tell him. Tina's feelings illustrate

    (A) transference   (D) free association

    (B) insight   (E) the placebo effect

    (C) resistance

82. Which therapeutic approach focuses on clients discovering their own ways to resolve their issues?

(A) Psychoanalytic   (D) Client-centered

(B) Gestalt   (E) Medical

(C) Cognitive

83. Systematic desensitization would involve

(A) anti-psychotic drugs

(B) associating relaxation with anxiety-arousing situations

(C) challenging client's irrational thoughts

(D) helping a client understand his or her "self"

(E) pairing unpleasant experiences with undesirable behaviors

84. Bill, who's depressed, recently succeeded in getting a job he very much wanted. A cognitive therapist would want Bill to attribute his success to

(A) Bill's own talent and ability

(B) the therapist's support

(C) luck

(D) his future boss's low standards

(E) the way Bill's parents raised him

85. A first-grade teacher gives his students gold stars when they read on their own during classroom "free time." When they get 10 stars, they can spend their free time playing outside. What technique for behavior change is this teacher using?

(A) Counter-conditioning

(B) Flooding

(C) Free association

(D) Systematic desensitization

(E) A token economy

86. Which of these people is most likely to be prescribed Thorazine?

(A) Tommy, who's depressed

(B) Art, who can't remember anything 15 minutes prior to an accident he was in

(C) Gilda, who suffers from delusions of persecution

(D) Lloyd, who has mood swings

(E) Terry, who's agoraphobic

87. Karen insisted that her boyfriend was late getting to her house because he never pays attention to what time it is. Karen's explanation of her boyfriend's behavior is an example of

(A) a situational attribution

(B) in-group bias

(C) a dispositional attribution

(D) the bystander effect

(E) scapegoating

88. The fundamental attribution error refers to the fact that people tend to underestimate the extent to which others' behavior is influenced by

(A) their abilities and skills

(B) genes

(C) motivational states

(D) personality traits

(E) situational factors

89. Which of the following illustrates that our behavior can change our attitudes?

(A) The foot-in-the-door phenomenon

(B) The bystander effect

(C) The mere exposure effect

(D) Social loafing

(E) Social facilitation

90. When our behavior is inconsistent with our attitudes or values, we feel a tension called

    (A) in-group bias   (D) groupthink

    (B) group polarization   (E) cognitive dissonance

    (C) deindividuation

91. Veronica is strongly in favor of serving liquor at the campus cafeteria. As part of a class debate on the topic, though, she freely generates arguments against serving liquor at the cafeteria. According to cognitive dissonance theory,

    (A) Veronica's classmates will now be more in favor of serving liquor at the cafeteria

    (B) Veronica's arguments won't persuade her classmates to change their views about serving liquor at the cafeteria

    (C) Veronica's view of serving liquor at the cafeteria won't change

    (D) Veronica will now be less in favor of serving liquor at the cafeteria

    (E) Veronica will now be more in favor of serving liquor at the cafeteria

92. Individualistic cultures are likely to promote

    (A) group polarization   (D) groupthink

    (B) social loafing   (E) in-group bias

    (C) non-conformity

93. Social facilitation involves

    (A) exerting less effort when doing a task as part of a group than by oneself

    (B) an individual performing better at a task when others are around

    (C) developing a liking for someone you run across frequently

    (D) the shift toward more extreme attitudes when groups of people with similar views discuss an issue

    (E) the tendency for people to conform to a large request after having already complied with a smaller request

94. Vera, Chuck, and Dave all think Paul is a relatively nice person. After talking together about why they think Paul is nice, though, they've all decided that Paul is so nice that he's one of the nicest persons on the planet. What is this phenomenon called?

    (A) Group polarization   (D) Deindividuation

    (B) Social facilitation   (E) The mere exposure effect

    (C) Cognitive dissonance

95. High school kids often believe that their own high school is better than any of the neighboring high schools. This illustrates

    (A) the fundamental attribution error

    (B) social facilitation

    (C) in-group bias

    (D) scapegoating

    (E) superordinate goals

96. In a famous study, college freshmen were paired randomly with someone of the opposite sex for a "Welcome Week" dance. What determined most whether individuals liked the person with whom they were paired?

    (A) Similarity in religious beliefs

    (B) What his/her major was

    (C) Where he/she was from

    (D) Similarity in intelligence

    (E) Physical attractiveness

97. An aptitude test that is supposed to measure how well people will do in sales and marketing jobs successfully predicts how well those who take it will do as real estate agents. This test has a high degree of

    (A) face validity   (D) construct validity

    (B) predictive validity   (E) standardization

    (C) content validity

98. Each person who completed a 14-item personality test is given a total score for ratings of odd-numbered items, as well as a total score for even-numbered items. The correlation between those two sets of scores is then computed. This procedure would be used to assess

    (A) construct validity   (D) split-half reliability

    (B) face validity   (E) criterion-related validity

    (C) test-retest reliability

99. The most commonly occurring score in a distribution of scores is called

    (A) the standard deviation

    (B) the mode

    (C) the mean

    (D) the arithmetic average

    (E) the median

100. In an experiment, the researcher manipulates teaching style in order to measure its effects on test scores for a biology class. It turns out that the average test score among subjects in the experimental group was 81 and the average score for subjects in the control group was 75. If that 6-point difference between those two groups were "statistically significant," what would that mean?

    (A) The difference between the two groups was 5%.

    (B) The two groups were different.

    (C) A difference as big as 6 points, or more, would be unlikely to happen by chance.

    (D) That 6-point difference is important.

    (E) The populations those samples came from must differ from each other, as well.

CLEP INTRODUCTORY PSYCHOLOGY
PRACTICE TEST 1

ANSWER KEY

1.	(C)	26.	(D)	51.	(D)	76.	(B)
2.	(E)	27.	(A)	52.	(C)	77.	(E)
3.	(A)	28.	(A)	53.	(B)	78.	(D)
4.	(B)	29.	(B)	54.	(E)	79.	(A)
5.	(E)	30.	(E)	55.	(A)	80.	(C)
6.	(D)	31.	(C)	56.	(C)	81.	(A)
7.	(C)	32.	(D)	57.	(D)	82.	(D)
8.	(A)	33.	(D)	58.	(C)	83.	(B)
9.	(D)	34.	(A)	59.	(C)	84.	(A)
10.	(A)	35.	(E)	60.	(A)	85.	(E)
11.	(B)	36.	(A)	61.	(D)	86.	(C)
12.	(B)	37.	(A)	62.	(B)	87.	(C)
13.	(B)	38.	(B)	63.	(E)	88.	(E)
14.	(A)	39.	(C)	64.	(E)	89.	(A)
15.	(D)	40.	(B)	65.	(B)	90.	(E)
16.	(D)	41.	(E)	66.	(A)	91.	(D)
17.	(C)	42.	(B)	67.	(C)	92.	(C)
18.	(D)	43.	(B)	68.	(B)	93.	(B)
19.	(B)	44.	(D)	69.	(E)	94.	(A)
20.	(B)	45.	(B)	70.	(A)	95.	(C)
21.	(A)	46.	(D)	71.	(D)	96.	(E)
22.	(B)	47.	(B)	72.	(E)	97.	(B)
23.	(E)	48.	(E)	73.	(B)	98.	(D)
24.	(E)	49.	(C)	74.	(A)	99.	(B)
25.	(E)	50.	(A)	75.	(C)	100.	(C)

DETAILED EXPLANATIONS OF ANSWERS

PRACTICE TEST 1

1.   **(C)**   Functionalists focus on the value that behaviors and other psychological characteristics have for an organism's adaptation to its environment. Structuralists focus on what those behaviors and characteristics are, and on finding the basic components that make them up.

2.   **(E)**   The biological perspective emphasizes the roles of hormones, neurotransmitters, and other biological and physiological agents in determining behavior. Psychoanalysts emphasize unconscious wishes and fears; behaviorists emphasize learning; humanists emphasize authenticity of one's self; and cognitivists emphasize thought processes.

3.   **(A)**   Using rewards (or reinforcers) and punishment to change behavior is called "operant conditioning." Operant conditioning is a form of learning, which is central to the behavioral approach to psychology.

4.   **(B)**   Experiments test cause-and-effect relationships by manipulating the presumed cause (the independent variable) and measuring the effect in terms of differences in behavior (the dependent variable) across the experimental and control groups.

5.   **(E)**   This researcher is watching ongoing behavior in a real-life setting without interfering with it or asking the subjects for information.

6.   **(D)**   Correlation coefficients provide two pieces of information: the direction of a relationship between two variables and the magnitude of that relationship. The magnitude can range from 0 to 1 and, regardless of the direction of the relationship, higher numbers indicate stronger relationships.

7. **(C)** Random assignment to treatment conditions ensures the average behavior of people in the experimental group wouldn't differ from the average behavior of those in the control group. Thus, following the experimental manipulation, any differences in behavior (the dependent variable) between the two groups would have to be due to the independent variable. The experimental treatment is represented by the independent variable, so subjects are equivalent with respect to that before the experiment regardless of whether they've been randomly assigned or not.

8. **(A)** "Nature" has to do with inborn, genetic, biological reasons for behavior, whereas "nurture" has to do with behaviors, or changes in behaviors, that are the product of experiences.

9. **(D)** The medulla is at the base of the brainstem, which is at the top of the spinal cord. The thalamus is at the top of the brainstem and the reticular formation is in the middle of the brainstem. The parietal lobe is at the back of the brain. The cerebellum hangs under the back of the brain behind the brainstem.

10. **(A)** Dendrites, axons, somas, and terminal buttons are parts of neurons.

11. **(B)** A myelin sheath is a layer of fatty tissue that insulates the axons of some neurons. Dendrites are a part of the neuron itself, as are vesicles. An action potential is the signal that passes down the neuron. Depolarization is one of the signal-related processes that is accelerated by having a myelin sheath on the neuron.

12. **(B)** The absolute refractory period is a resting pause during which neurons pump positively charged sodium ions back out.

13. **(B)** The central nervous system includes only the brain and spinal cord. The rest of the nervous system is called the peripheral nervous system and is divided into the somatic nervous system, which controls the voluntary movement of skeletal muscles, and the autonomic nervous system (which has two divisions: sympathetic and parasympathetic).

14. **(A)** Wernicke's area is the part of the brain in which acoustical codes—including spoken words—are decoded and interpreted. Broca's area, another brain structure involved in speech, is responsible for directing the muscle movements involved in speaking.

15. **(D)** The term "endorphin" is short for "endogenous morphine" (i.e., a painkiller produced in the body).

16. **(D)** Neurotransmitters are stored in terminal buttons on the neuron's axon where they're released to signal adjacent cells.

17. **(C)** Heart rate and breathing are regulated by the medulla; the hypothalamus controls hunger; the amygdala regulates fear and aggression; and voluntary movement is coordinated by the cerebellum.

18. **(D)** Perceptual processes (such as perception, top-down processing, subliminal perception) and parallel processing have to do with what happens after stimuli are sensed.

19. **(B)** Perception happens after detecting a stimulus. The just-noticeable difference (or difference threshold) is the smallest difference a person can detect between two stimuli. Feature detection has to do with specific neurons' abilities to detect particular features of a stimulus (e.g., lines or angles).

20. **(B)** Weber's Law says that our thresholds for distinguishing between two similar stimuli is a constant proportion of the size of the original stimulus.

21. **(A)** Transduction involves transforming one form of energy (such as light waves) into another form of energy (such as nerve impulses).

22. **(B)** Light energy strikes rods and cones: Rods enable black-and-white vision; cones enable color. That energy is transduced into signals sent along bipolar cells and ganglion cells. Ganglion fibers make up the optic nerve, which carries information to the brain. (Something "auditory" has to do with hearing, not vision.)

23. **(E)** Convergence has to do with the extent to which your eyes must turn inward in order to focus on an object (less convergence is a cue to greater distance). The other cues are based on what only one eye can see.

24. **(E)** Linear perspective is a monocular cue to distance. The more that two lines converge, the greater their perceived distance. Retinal disparity is the difference between two images on your two retinas; relative

motion is the perception that objects closer than a fixation point seem to move backwards (relative to the fixation point); a texture gradient, from coarse to smooth, is a cue to increasing distance; and when one object blocks another (interposition), it appears closer.

25. **(E)** Shape constancy is the ability to recognize an object when seeing it from a new angle; linear perspective is a monocular cue to distance; perceptual adaptation is the ability to adjust to novel sensory input; and a perceptual set is a predisposition to interpret stimuli in a particular way.

26. **(D)** "Circadian" is from the Latin for "about" (i.e., circa) and "day" (i.e., dies), so it means "about the day," or a 24-hour period.

27. **(A)** Just prior to entering the first stage of sleep, the brain produces relatively slow, regular waves called alpha waves. Sleep spindles occur during Stage 2 sleep; delta waves are long, slow waves that occur during Stage 4 sleep; and rapid eye movements occur during REM sleep.

28. **(A)** Sensations of falling or floating, called hypnogogic sensations, occur during the five minutes or so of light sleep, just as one has fallen asleep.

29. **(B)** Stage 1 sleep lasts about 5 minutes, Stage 2 lasts about 20 minutes, Stage 3 is several minutes long, and Stage 4 lasts about 30 minutes; the next half hour is spent returning through Stage 3 and Stage 2 sleep, and then entering a period of REM sleep. Stage 4 gets shorter with each cycle, whereas REM sleep gets longer.

30. **(E)** Sleep apnea involves trouble breathing, and trouble getting to sleep or staying asleep is insomnia.

31. **(C)** The social influence theory of hypnosis says that people who have been hypnotized are simply fulfilling a social role—that of a good hypnotized subject—and so their behavior while hypnotized reflects normal, everyday psychological processes.

32. **(D)** In classical conditioning, learning has to do with figuring out relationships between or among stimuli; in its simplest form, a conditioned stimulus is paired with an unconditioned stimulus. In operant conditioning, a relationship between one's behavior (a response) and its consequences (a stimulus) is learned.

33. **(D)**   In classical conditioning, learning is evidenced by the appearance of a particular response (like sneezing) to a stimulus that hadn't produced it before (Anita).

34. **(A)**   Because cat fur automatically and reflexively produces the relevant response (sneezing), it must be the unconditioned stimulus (and sneezing must be the unconditioned response).

35. **(E)**   Wally didn't learn to sneeze in response to cat fur, but apparently did learn to sneeze in response to Anita. When cat fur causes his sneezing, then, that sneezing is an unconditioned response; when Anita causes his sneezing, that sneezing would be a conditioned response.

36. **(A)**   When a conditioned stimulus (Anita) shows up without an unconditioned stimulus (in this case, cat fur), the learned behavior begins to go away, or extinguish. If after the CR were extinguished Anita went away for a while, Wally would be likely to sneeze when she came back (spontaneous recovery).

37. **(A)**   A stimulus that's a) presented and b) desirable shows up after Bob does something that sells a magazine. That would feel good. Any consequence that feels good must be reinforcement and, if it involves a stimulus being presented, it must be positive.

38. **(B)**   Lori's behavior (drinking wine) is followed by the removal of a stimulus (making the consequence "negative") that is unpleasant (i.e., stress). This feels good, so it must be reinforcement.

39. **(C)**   Jeff's winning depended on how many responses he made (that is, how many tickets he bought), so this is a ratio schedule, but the number of responses needed varied from one win to the next, so it's a variable schedule. Here's a tip: On an interval schedule, the odds of getting reinforced go up with the mere passage of time (that doesn't happen with any form of gambling).

40. **(B)**   This situation illustrates the method of successive approximations, or shaping. In this case, it took five minutes of whining for Lucy to get her first reinforcement, then 10 minutes (which more closely "approximates" 20 minutes), then 20 minutes (which more closely approximates some longer period of time), and so forth.

41. **(E)** Vicarious learning is also called "social learning," "observational learning," or "modeling." The idea is that learning happens when people mentally represent the contingency between a behavior and its consequence, even without doing the behavior or experiencing the consequence themselves. Sally learned that hitting would produce punishment (a contingency) by seeing that contingency enforced for someone else.

42. **(B)** A heuristic is a mental shortcut for solving problems (e.g., "always look for National Public Radio at the low end of the FM dial first"). Algorithms are step-by-step, methodical solutions; a prototype is an ideal example of a category; insight is a flash of inspiration, rather than a strategy; and fixations interfere with solving problems.

43. **(B)** Belief perseverance involves maintaining one's beliefs (in this case, that Dave is shy) in the face of evidence that they're not true (Dave's outgoing behavior at several subsequent meetings).

44. **(D)** Telegraphic speech is a one- or two-word "sentence" which is accompanied by gestures and expressions that fill in the speaker's intentions.

45. **(B)** By 12 months of age, children are essentially deaf to sounds that aren't used in their native language (unless they've been exposed to those sounds).

46. **(D)** "Distributed practice" involves studying manageable amounts of material for relatively short periods of time, but doing it consistently day after day. This capitalizes on the spacing effect: Information is remembered better when rehearsal is distributed over time than when spaced out or crammed into a short period of time.

47. **(B)** Implicit memory is also called "procedural memory," whereas explicit, or declarative, memory involves being aware of what you know. A brief photographic memory of an image is called iconic memory; a brief memory of an auditory stimulus is called echoic memory. Flashbulb memories are vivid memories of emotionally charged events. Working memory is another term for "short-term memory."

48. **(E)** The Stanford-Binet defined the intelligence quotient as follows: mental age divided by chronological age, multiplied by 100. In this case, then: 8 divided by 10, times 100.

49. **(C)** The ability to do well is measured with aptitude tests; the ability to learn is presumably a function of intelligence; personality tests measure differences in traits.

50. **(A)** Drives, incentives, motives, and emotions don't necessarily produce patterns of behavior that are invariant and universal across members of a species; for example, people can learn unique ways of responding to these forces.

51. **(D)** Needs trigger an urge without external incentives like rewards or the avoidance of punishment, and one type of need might be for arousal.

52. **(C)** *Cathexis* is a mental or emotional attachment, whether conscious or unconscious, to a person, object, or idea. The "Big Five" ("Five-Factor Model") traits are openness, conscientiousness, extraversion, agreeableness, and neuroticism. Organizing the subject matter into these broad categories is a taxonomic convenience.

53. **(B)** The sexual response cycle includes the excitement phase (producing signs of sexual arousal), the plateau phase (increased arousal), orgasm, and a resolution phase (loss of arousal). The refractory period occurs during this resolution phase.

54. **(E)** Cannon-Bard argued that arousal and emotion occur simultaneously. Schacter's two-factor theory states that a cognitive label for arousal is necessary to have an emotional experience.

55. **(A)** In this example, the emotion being experienced depends on how the arousal has been interpreted. The Cannon-Bard and James-Lange theories consider emotions to be linked to specific patterns of arousal. Neither instinct theory nor opponent-process theory explains the effects of arousal from caffeine on emotional intensity.

56. **(C)** In general, high levels of arousal interfere with performance at a task, and low levels of arousal undermine attention and effort (so performance suffers). But the optimal level of arousal varies for different sorts of tasks: For easy tasks high arousal improves performance, whereas for difficult tasks low arousal improves performance.

57. **(D)** In part, happiness depends on doing better than we think other people are doing (thus the expression, "relative deprivation"). James-

Lange, opponent-process theory, and two-factor theory don't (easily) account for emotions being a function of comparisons with other people; the adaptation-level phenomenon has to do with a reduction in happiness as one habituates to some consistent level of wealth (or some other desirable stimulus).

58. **(C)**   The union of a sperm and ovum is a zygote; when the zygote implants itself in the uterine wall (at about two weeks after conception) it's called an embryo; when hard bone begins to form (about 8 weeks) it's called a fetus.

59. **(C)**   "Age is confounded with cohort" means that differences across age groups could be due to aging itself or to differences in the time periods in which subjects grew up. In cross-sectional studies, subjects of different ages (and, so, cohorts) are tested at the same time. In longitudinal studies, all subjects are from the same cohort, so differences in cohorts can't be responsible for differences across ages.

60. **(A)**   Tim interpreted what he saw in terms of his current understanding of animals (i.e., he assimilated). Had he changed his understanding of animals ("horses and zebras are different") he would have been accommodating.

61. **(D)**   Conservation is the understanding that quantitative aspects of an object, such as its mass, don't necessarily change when its appearance changes: There's the same amount of trash, it just looks different. When Samantha assimilates, and then accommodates, that fact, she'll have achieved the ability to conserve. Being able to conserve will happen with or without Samantha being egocentric, and none of this would require formal operational thinking.

62. **(B)**   Imprinting, which does contribute to attachment in some species, happens during a critical period early in life. The attachment, however, can form between the infant and any stimulus that happens to be around at the "right" time, not just between the infant and a caregiver.

63. **(E)**   According to Erikson, adolescents face the task of integrating the various social roles they fill, as well as the various talents, abilities, and skills they may have, into one coherent personality.

64. **(E)**   Pre-conventional morality is based on doing what will get tangible rewards and not doing what will get punished. Conventional morality involves upholding laws and rules just because they're laws and rules. Post-conventional morality is based on one's own abstract ethical principles.

65. **(B)**   The ability to recall newly learned material declines with age, but the ability to recognize material that has recently been learned is stable.

66. **(A)**   When intelligence is defined as information that one has accumulated over a lifetime (i.e., crystallized intelligence), intelligence increases with age; when it's defined as the ability to reason abstractly and quickly (i.e., fluid intelligence), it tends to decline in late adulthood.

67. **(C)**   Superego operates according to the morality principle: Do what's right and don't do what's wrong, regardless of the consequences.

68. **(B)**   Because ego is the only part of personality that's realistic, and flexible, part of its job is to get needs met in a realistic way. In part, that means resolving conflicts between opposing ways of behaving. Id and superego are inflexible and unrealistic.

69. **(E)**   Regression involves returning to an earlier way of behaving (e.g., an older child or adult throwing a temper tantrum, like a child); rationalizing involves attempts to justify irrational behavior with rational arguments; projecting is attributing characteristics you don't like in yourself to other people; and reaction formations involve doing the opposite of what you really want to do.

70. **(A)**   Traits are patterns of behavior (e.g., expressing extraverted behavior in many ways across many situations) that describe dimensions along which people differ (e.g., anywhere from no extraversion to extremely high extraversion).

71. **(D)**   The three components of the personality, according to Rogers, are the self-concept, ideal self, and actual self, and one's goal in life to integrate these three components. Id, conscience, and superego are important Freudian concepts, and the collective unconscious is a Jungian concept.

72. **(E)** The term "reciprocal determinism" describes the ways in which social factors, personality, and one's own behavior can interact to determine future behavior.

73. **(B)** Having multiple personalities (if such a thing actually exists) is called "dissociative identity disorder." (Schizophrenia involves a break from reality; one could have several personalities, each of which can deal with reality, and thus not be schizophrenic.)

74. **(A)** People who are antisocial violate others' rights and property without guilt or remorse. Narcissists have fantasies of success and fame, wanting others to treat them as someone important; schizophrenia involves difficulty distinguishing between reality and fantasy; dissociative disorders involve the fragmentation of personality; and obsessive-compulsive disorder is an anxiety disorder involving repetitive patterns of thoughts or behaviors.

75. **(C)** Anxiety disorders are characterized by feelings of distress and anxiety. An intense, irrational fear with a specific focus would be a phobia; in Larry's case, the anxiety is "free floating."

76. **(B)** Obsessive-compulsive disorder involves repetitive thoughts (obsessions) and behaviors (compulsions) that often revolve around neatness or germs.

77. **(E)** Dissociative disorders involve the fragmentation of personality. In Larry's case, he has an "old" self, of which he apparently has no memory, but also a "new" self, around which his current life revolves.

78. **(D)** Catatonia is characterized chiefly by excessive, purposeless movement or by immobility, but might also involve waxy flexibility, echolalia, or echopraxia.

79. **(A)** A conversion disorder involves the "conversion" of a psychological conflict ("My parents fight and I can't do anything about it") into a physical symptom (not being able to hear) that eliminates the conflict.

80. **(C)** Psychoanalysts rely on this technique as a way to get patients past their resistance to talking about anxiety-provoking issues and memories.

81. **(A)** Tina is "transferring" feeling from a previous relationship (with her father) to her therapist.

82. **(D)** Rogerian, client-centered therapy is non-directive because it assumes that everyone (clients included) has the capacity for self-actualizing.

83. **(B)** Systematic desensitization is based on principles of classical conditioning. Phobic objects presumably arouse anxiety (as a conditioned response) because they've been paired in the past with something that unconditionally aroused anxiety. By pairing them with situations in which the client relaxes, they should come to produce a new conditioned response—relaxation.

84. **(A)** Depressed people tend to attribute their own failures to internal, stable characteristics ("I'm dumb") while attributing their successes to external factors (e.g., an easy test). By changing the way that Bill explains his failures and successes, his depression could be lessened or eliminated.

85. **(E)** In token economies, people are given tokens of some sort that have little inherent value (e.g., gold stars) and can exchange those tokens for tangible rewards.

86. **(C)** Chlorpromazine (sold as Thorazine) is an anti-psychotic drug used to treat people with hallucinations or delusions.

87. **(C)** Karen has explained her boyfriend's behavior in terms of something internal (i.e., internal to him, as an "actor"): what he's like, a trait, a "disposition."

88. **(E)** The fundamental attribution error describes people's tendency to explain other people's behavior in terms of dispositions rather than situations. People tend to explain their own behavior, though, in terms of situations.

89. **(A)** The compliance produced when making a large request after originally getting compliance with a smaller request is called the foot-in-the-door phenomenon. When people comply with the smaller request (e.g., loaning someone a pencil), they may come to see themselves as the type of person who complies with that sort of request (or maybe they just see themselves as helpful), and so are more likely to comply with the larger

request later (e.g., loaning someone their lecture notes from a class) because doing so would be consistent with their new view of themselves.

90. **(E)** According to cognitive dissonance theory, dissonance is a state of discomfort that people will relieve by changing a pre-existing attitude so that it's consistent with a behavior they can't undo.

91. **(D)** Veronica's freely chosen behavior (generating arguments against serving liquor) is inconsistent with a pre-existing attitude (her favorable view of serving liquor). This should produce dissonance, which can then be reduced by changing her attitude so that it's more consistent with her behavior.

92. **(C)** Individualistic cultures value independence from groups. Collectivist cultures value teamwork and conformity at the expense of individual identity.

93. **(B)** The presence of others (especially those in a position to evaluate one's performance) often produces arousal, which can enhance performance on easy or well-learned tasks (although it interferes with performance on difficult tasks). The other answer options describe social loafing, mere exposure, group polarization, and the foot-in-the-door phenomenon, respectively.

94. **(A)** Group polarization happens when people discuss a topic about which they have similar opinions. There is a tendency for their opinions to become more extreme.

95. **(C)** When people are organized into groups, even at random or without a purpose, they tend to favor those within their own group.

96. **(E)** At least after just a first meeting, at the dance, these students were more likely to want another date with someone who they considered attractive than with someone they didn't.

97. **(B)** Having predictive validity (or criterion-related validity) means that scores on a test are predictive of the sorts of behaviors those test scores should be related to. For example, how well one does as a real-estate agent, which is a sales job, should be related to scores on a sales and marketing test. Face validity, also called content validity, is about whether test items look like they'd measure what they're supposed to; construct

validity is about whether scores on a test are related to scores on other tests in meaningful ways.

98. **(D)** Construct validity is about whether scores on a test are related to scores on other tests in meaningful ways; face validity is about whether test items look like they'd measure what they're supposed to; test-retest reliability is determined by giving the same test twice (not splitting one test in half); and criterion-related validity means that scores on a test are predictive of related behaviors.

99. **(B)** The standard deviation is a measure of how widely dispersed scores are around the mean; the mean is the arithmetic average (the sum of the scores, divided by the number of scores that were summed); and the median is the score below which (or above which) 50% of scores in the distribution fall.

100. **(C)** A statistically significant difference between two samples (i.e., the experimental and control groups) is one that would be unlikely to happen by chance (if the difference in the populations the samples came from is zero). Even small and trivial differences can, under some circumstances, be statistically significant. The groups can differ without that difference being statistically significant, and any statistically significant difference could have happened by chance (i.e., the populations might not really differ).

▼

PRACTICE
TEST 2

This test is also on CD-ROM in our special interactive CLEP Introductory Psychology TEST*ware*®. It is highly recommended that you first take this exam on computer. You will then have the additional study features and benefits of enforced timed conditions, individual diagnostic analysis, and instant scoring. See page ix for guidance on how to get the most out of our CLEP Introductory Psychology software.

CLEP INTRODUCTORY PSYCHOLOGY

Practice Test 2

(Answer sheets appear in the back of this book.)

TIME: 90 Minutes
            100 Questions

DIRECTIONS: Each of the questions or incomplete statements below is followed by five possible answers or completions. Select the best choice in each case and fill in the corresponding oval on the answer sheet.

---

1. Which theoretical approach is concerned with how an organism uses its perceptual abilities to function in its environment?

    (A) Humanistic   (D) Existentialist

    (B) Functionalist   (E) Structuralist

    (C) Behaviorist

2. Which school of psychology argues that only behaviors that can be observed directly should be studied?

    (A) Humanism   (D) Functionalism

    (B) Psychoanalysis   (E) Behaviorism

    (C) Structuralism

3. Which approach to psychology focuses on thought processes?

    (A) Biological   (B) Behavioral

(C) Cognitive   (D) Humanistic

(E) Psychodynamic

4. Subjects know that their behavior is being observed in the typical settings for all of the following research methods EXCEPT

(A) Case study

(B) Naturalistic observation

(C) Survey

(D) Correlational

(E) Experimental

5. Which research method involves studying the behavior of individuals one at a time and in depth?

(A) Case study

(B) Naturalistic observation

(C) Survey

(D) Correlational

(E) Experimental

6. In order to study the effects of music on memory, a researcher has one group of subjects listen to music while studying a list of words and another group study the same list without listening to music. In this experiment, the number or words each subject can remember would be

(A) the independent variable

(B) a placebo

(C) manipulated by the experimenter

(D) the dependent variable

(E) a confounding variable

7. A set of principles that organizes and explains known facts, as well as predicting new ones, is called a(n)

(A) hypothesis   (B) experiment

(C) theory   (D) assumption

(E) operational definition

8. Random samples are ones in which

(A) subjects all share the same characteristics

(B) the number of subjects is determined by chance

(C) subjects don't differ on the dependent variable

(D) everyone in the population had an equal chance of being included

(E) subjects volunteered to participate

9. The parasympathetic nervous system would have which of the following effects?

(A) Raising blood sugar

(B) Producing perspiration

(C) Inhibiting digestion

(D) Slowing heart rate

(E) Dilating the pupils of the eye

10. In which lobe of the brain is the visual cortex found?

(A) Temporal   (D) Frontal

(B) Occipital   (E) Association areas

(C) Parietal

11. Which of the following is often called the master gland?

(A) Thyroid   (D) Ovaries/Testes

(B) Adrenal   (E) Pituitary

(C) Pancreas

12. The resting potential for a neuron is

(A) 0 mV   (D) – 40 mV

(B) 40 mV   (E) –70 mV

(C) 70 mV

13. A neuron can receive signals through its

    (A) soma   (D) nucleus

    (B) Axon   (E) dendrites

    (C) Terminal buttons

14. Which section of the brain translates thoughts into speech?

    (A) Wernicke's area   (D) Broca's area

    (B) Occipital lobe   (E) Parietal lobe

    (C) Corpus callosum

15. Neurons are held together and provided with nutrients by

    (A) neurotransmitters   (D) serotonin

    (B) hormones   (E) dopamine

    (C) glia cells

16. What is the most common inhibitor in the brain, and may have something to do with eating and sleeping disorders?

    (A) Acetylcholine   (D) Norepinephrine

    (B) GABA   (E) Serotonin

    (C) Dopamine

17. Patients with severe seizures sometimes have which part of their brain disconnected from other parts?

    (A) Thalamus   (D) Frontal lobes

    (B) Limbic system   (E) Hypothalamus

    (C) Corpus callosum

18. Perception is the process by which

    (A) sensory stimulation is made meaningful

    (B) energy originating from stimuli is detected

    (C) stimulus energy is transformed into neural energy

    (D) specific features of objects are detected

    (E) sensory adaptation occurs

19. The minimum amount of energy required to produce a sensation is called

    (A) the just-noticeable difference

    (B) the absolute threshold

    (C) the difference threshold

    (D) feature detection

    (E) the energy threshold

20. The process of converting sound waves into neural impulses is called

    (A) accommodation   (D) feature detection

    (B) top-down processing   (E) transduction

    (C) parallel processing

21. The amount of light entering the eye is controlled by the

    (A) optic nerve   (D) iris

    (B) retina   (E) cochlea

    (C) lens

22. Perceiving an object as distinct from its surroundings is called

    (A) shape constancy

    (B) figure-ground perception

    (C) the phi phenomenon

    (D) a perceptual set

    (E) sensation

23. That you would see the letter "N" as a single stimulus instead of three distinct lines illustrates the principle of

    (A) continuity   (D) closure

    (B) convergence   (E) depth perception

    (C) shape constancy

24. The extent to which your eyes must turn inward (toward your nose) to view an object is called

    (A) size constancy   (D) closure

    (B) interposition   (E) motion parallax

    (C) convergence

25. A stereotype is a form of

    (A) telepathy   (D) fixation point

    (B) binocular cue   (E) perceptual set

    (C) sensation

26. As daytime approaches, our body temperatures typically rise. This illustrates the effects of

    (A) dreaming   (D) paradoxical sleep

    (B) delta waves   (E) REM rebound

    (C) the circadian rhythm

27. A feeling of falling or floating when drifting off to sleep is called

    (A) apnea   (D) narcolepsy

    (B) paradoxical sleep   (E) a sleep spindle

    (C) a hypnogogic sensation

28. Sleep spindles

    (A) occur during Stage 1 sleep

    (B) are long, slow brain waves

    (C) are characterized by alpha waves

    (D) are rapid, rhythmic bursts of brain activity

    (E) are characterized by delta waves

29. A sleep disorder involving an interruption in breathing is called

    (A) sleep apnea   (D) REM rebound

    (B) narcolepsy   (E) hypnosis

    (C) insomnia

30. Which of the following drugs would be used as a tranquilizer?

    (A) Opiates   (D) Hallucinogens

    (B) Barbiturates   (E) Anti-psychotics

    (C) Amphetamines

31. Which of the following would be considered a psychedelic drug?

    (A) Cocaine   (D) Heroin

    (B) Marijuana   (E) LSD

    (C) THC

32. Habituation is an example of

    (A) sensitization

    (B) non-associative learning

    (C) associative learning

    (D) an instrumental behavior

    (E) modeling

33. Which of the following is an unconditioned response?

    (A) Opening the door to get into your house

    (B) A dog coming when it's called

    (C) The watering of your eye when a piece of dirt gets in it

    (D) Cutting your fingernails

    (E) Hitting someone who has insulted you

34. In Pavlov's studies with dogs, a bell was rung and then the dog was given food. Eventually, the dog salivated when hearing the bell. In these studies, the bell was a(n)

    (A) secondary reinforcer

    (B) negative reinforcer

    (C) conditioned stimulus

    (D) unconditioned stimulus

    (E) conditioned response

35. Larry was bitten by a mouse when he was little and so learned to fear mice. But he is also afraid of other furry rodents. Larry's fear of stimuli that are similar to, but not the same as, the one involved in his learning is the product of

    (A) latent learning   (D) generalization

    (B) shaping   (E) discrimination

    (C) operant conditioning

36. A conditioned stimulus is presented by itself, without the unconditioned stimulus, until the conditioned response goes away. The next day, though, the conditioned stimulus produces the conditioned response a few times before the response again goes away. This temporary return of an extinguished conditioned response is called

    (A) spontaneous recovery   (D) the overjustification effect

    (B) generalization   (E) operant conditioning

    (C) discrimination

37. Negative reinforcement is exemplified by which of the following?

    (A) Getting money for good behavior

    (B) Getting money for bad behavior

    (C) Losing a toy for bad behavior

    (D) A child avoiding punishment when it lies about its behavior

    (E) Getting a spanking

38. When her parents started rewarding her for playing the piano, Nicki went from playing for three hours a week to playing 10 hours a week. When they stopped reinforcing her, though, Nicki began playing only one hour a week. This reduction in the time spent playing after having been reinforced for it is called

    (A) shaping   (D) extinction

    (B) response-cost training   (E) the overjustification effect

    (C) discrimination

39. Councilman Sanders comes up for re-election every two years and has been in office for 18 years. A month before every election he goes door-to-door in his district visiting potential voters. For the rest of his term he ignores the people in his district and they ignore him. On which schedule of reinforcement has Councilman Sanders' visits to the voters been reinforced?

    (A) Fixed ratio

    (B) Variable ratio

    (C) A continuous reinforcement

    (D) Fixed interval

    (E) Variable interval

40. In his first two years of college, Bill did well when he took history classes but not when he took political science classes. Now, in his last two years, he's taking more history classes but not taking any political science. What is Bill's preference for a reinforced activity over a non-reinforced one called?

    (A) Latent learning

    (B) Discrimination

    (C) Overjustification

    (D) Respondent conditioning

    (E) Generalization

41. The learning procedure that involves reinforcing successively closer approximations to a desired behavior is called

    (A) discrimination

    (B) modeling

    (C) generalization

    (D) shaping

    (E) intermittent reinforcement

42. The bias toward thinking of objects only in terms of their normal uses, instead of some novel use for which they might be needed, is called

(A) the availability heuristic

(B) the representativeness heuristic

(C) functional fixedness

(D) confirmation bias

(E) belief perseverance

43. People are likely to overestimate the percentage of lawsuits that go to trial, as opposed to being settled out of court, because lawsuits that go to trial are more memorable than those that don't. This phenomenon is called

(A) the representativeness heuristic

(B) overconfidence

(C) confirmation bias

(D) the framing effect

(E) the availability heuristic

44. The area of language that deals with linking words to the objects and ideas they represent is

(A) semantics

(B) syntax

(C) pragmatics

(D) phonetics

(E) telegraphic speech

45. Which stage of speech begins at about 3 or 4 months of age?

(A) The babbling stage

(B) The one-word stage

(C) The two-word stage

(D) The three-word stage

(E) The multiple-word stage

46. To better remember the names of the five Great Lakes you might use the acronym HOMES (Huron, Ontario, Michigan, Erie, Superior). This is an example of

(A) chunking

(B) rehearsal

(C) automatic processing

(D) flashbulb memory

(E) the serial-position effect

47. When given a list of names, which ones are you most likely to remember?

    (A) Those at the beginning of the list

    (B) Those in the middle of the list

    (C) Those at the end of the list

    (D) Those at the beginning and at the end

    (E) They should all be equally memorable

48. What kind of test is aimed at measuring how well someone might learn a specific skill?

    (A) Personality   (D) Standardized

    (B) Achievement   (E) Intelligence

    (C) Aptitude

49. The means by which you're able to determine how well you've done on a test compared to other people who have taken the same test is known as

    (A) validity   (D) factor analysis

    (B) reliability   (E) standardization

    (C) a correlational study

50. When you're thirsty, drinking water will reduce

    (A) achievement motivation

    (B) an instinct

    (C) a drive

    (D) extrinsic motivation

    (E) homeostasis

51. All of the following factors have been shown to affect the desire to affiliate EXCEPT

    (A) hunger   (D) fear

    (B) birth order   (E) intelligence

    (C) uncertainty

52. Which theory would be most useful for explaining why people would parachute from airplanes?

    (A) Theory X

    (B) Homeostasis

    (C) Instinct theory

    (D) Drive-reduction theory

    (E) Arousal theory

53. The most basic need in Maslow's hierarchy of needs is

    (A) self-actualization

    (B) belongingness

    (C) nourishment

    (D) security

    (E) self-esteem

54. According to the Cannon-Bard theory of emotion, which of the following is true?

    (A) Emotional behavior is always learned, not innate.

    (B) The experience of emotion causes physiological arousal.

    (C) Arousal and the subjective experience of emotion are triggered simultaneously by an emotion-arousing stimulus.

    (D) One must label one's arousal in order to have an emotional experience.

    (E) One must be aware of one's physiological arousal in order to experience emotion.

55. When Debbie was late for a test, she felt her heart racing and decided she was scared. When an attractive man asked her out she felt her heart racing and decided she was in love. Which theory explains this difference in her emotional responses?

    (A) James-Lange

    (B) Cannon-Bard

    (C) Instinct theory

    (D) Two-factor theory

    (E) Opponent-process theory

56. A high level of arousal would be most likely to interfere with someone's ability to

    (A) understand the instruction manual for a complex software program

    (B) sweep the kitchen

(C) watch television

(D) ride a bike

(E) get dressed

57. The idea that anger could be reduced by performing an aggressive behavior is called

(A) social learning

(B) disinhibition

(C) the adaptation-level principle

(D) two-factor theory

(E) the catharsis hypothesis

58. In the expression, "nature vs. nurture," the two terms refer respectively to

(A) biological factors and one's genetic make-up

(B) learning and environmental factors

(C) environmental factors and one's upbringing

(D) biological factors and environmental factors

(E) learning and genetic predispositions

59. Four-year-old Steve thinks his mother knows what he's doing, even though she's a hundred miles away and only talking to him on the phone. According to Piaget, which cognitive process accounts for Steve's ideas about what his mother knows?

(A) Accommodation   (D) Concrete operational thought

(B) Assimilation   (E) Conservation

(C) Egocentrism

60. The term "gender role" refers to

(A) the behaviors that are expected of men and women in a given culture

(B) one's sense of being male or female

(C) one's sexual orientation

(D) a person's biological sex

(E) the learning of sex-appropriate behavior

61. During which of Piaget's stages of development should a child come to understand that there can be as much pie in two small pieces as in one big one?

(A) Sensorimotor

(B) Pre-operational

(C) Concrete operational

(D) Formal operational

(E) Pre-conventional

62. What kind of parent is most likely to have children who feel good about themselves and are capable of taking care of themselves?

(A) Un-responsive

(B) Authoritarian

(C) Disengaged

(D) Permissive

(E) Authoritative

63. According to Erik Erikson, once a sense of identity has been achieved, young adults begin to search for

(A) trust

(B) intimacy

(C) competence

(D) autonomy

(E) integrity

64. Charlie won't make fun of other kids because he wants his teachers to like him. Which of Kohlberg's stages of moral development is Charlie in?

(A) Conventional

(B) Pre-conventional

(C) Formal operational

(D) Pre-operational

(E) Post-conventional

65. A group of first-graders is administered a battery of psychological tests every three years until they're 30 years old. What type of study is this?

(A) Experimental

(B) Cross sectional

(C) Cross-lagged

(D) Longitudinal

(E) Cross-sequential

66. How quickly and abstractly you're able to reason is referred to as

    (A) concrete operational thought

    (B) fluid intelligence

    (C) crystallized intelligence

    (D) egocentrism

    (E) temperament

67. According to Freud's psychoanalytic theory, behavior is driven by needs for what two things?

    (A) Genuineness and acceptance

    (B) Unconditional positive regard and empathy

    (C) Self-expression and self-actualization

    (D) Sex and aggression

    (E) Congruence and self-actualization

68. Jill is angry at her husband, but is behaving in unusually loving and kind ways toward him. Which defense mechanism is Jill using to hide her anger?

    (A) Reaction formation   (D) Identification

    (B) Projection   (E) Rationalization

    (C) Regression

69. Jim leaves his apartment in a mess and isn't respectful of his boss's authority. In which stage of development would Freud say Jim was fixated?

    (A) Oral   (D) Latency

    (B) Anal   (E) Genital

    (C) Phallic

70. According to research on self-perception, people tend to

    (A) take more responsibility for their failures than their successes

    (B) have unrealistically low self-esteem

    (C) see themselves as better in comparison to others

(D) be irrationally pessimistic about their futures

(E) think worse of themselves than they logically should

71. Mark believes that there's not much he can do to make good things happen for him or to keep bad things from happening to him. Mark's beliefs illustrate

(A) reciprocal determinism

(B) a self-serving bias

(C) a reaction formation

(D) conditions of worth

(E) external locus of control

72. Which approach to studying personality has as one of its goals reducing all traits down to smaller set of traits that describe most of the differences in people's behavior?

(A) Psychoanalytic   (D) Trait

(B) Humanistic   (E) Person-centered

(C) Social-cognitive

73. Whenever they watch television together, Wendy ignores what her husband says but then asks him to repeat it later. She agreed to keep the gas tank in their car full, but doesn't do it. She's also very slow getting up in the morning, which means her husband is the only one who ever gets their kids ready for school. When her husband complains, Wendy accuses him of being petty. Which personality disorder does Wendy have?

(A) Borderline   (D) Obsessive-compulsive

(B) Anti-social   (E) Passive-aggressive

(C) Narcissistic

74. After feeling suicidal and hopeless, and having disturbed appetite and sleeping patterns for several weeks, Linda has become energetic and optimistic, and exhibits fast speech, risk taking, and unsteady flow of ideas. This cycle has repeated itself many times over the last few years. Which disorder does Linda have?

(A) Bi-polar   (D) Dissociative identity

(B) Major depressive   (E) Obsessive-compulsive

(C) Generalized anxiety

75. Barbara thinks she's Queen Victoria. Furthermore, she thinks the CIA is eavesdropping on her phone conversations. Which form of schizophrenia does Barbara have?

(A) Paranoid   (D) Residual

(B) Catatonic   (E) Disorganized

(C) Undifferentiated

76. Hearing voices, when there are no voices to be heard, would be called which of the following?

(A) Phobia   (D) Hallucination

(B) Neurosis   (E) Delusion

(C) Conversion disorder

77. Someone with an avoidant personality disorder would also be likely to have

(A) an inflated sense of his or her importance

(B) no sense of guilt or shame

(C) a fear of being rejected by others

(D) delusions of grandeur

(E) overblown displays of emotion

78. Chronically low levels of energy, feelings of sadness, and low self-esteem that last at least two years are characteristic of

(A) a conversion reaction

(B) dysthymic disorder

(C) paranoid delusions

(D) dissociative disorders

(E) obsessive-compulsive disorder

79. An intense fear of a specific object would be called a(n)

    (A) generalized anxiety disorder

    (B) phobia

    (C) hallucination

    (D) compulsion

    (E) obsession

80. Kim abruptly stopped a therapy session by claiming she was nauseous and running out of the room. She did this just when her therapist asked her to discuss her unhappy relationship with her mother. Kim's behavior is likely to be interpreted as a sign of

    (A) catharsis

    (B) a reaction formation

    (C) insight

    (D) free association

    (E) resistance

81. Which type of therapy is most likely to focus on the patient's or client's childhood experiences?

    (A) Behavior modification

    (B) Bio-medical therapy

    (C) Client-centered therapy

    (D) Psychoanalysis

    (E) Rational-emotive therapy

82. When phobias are interpreted within a classical conditioning framework, the problem behavior is considered to be a(n)

    (A) conditioned response

    (B) unconditioned response

    (C) operant behavior

    (D) unconditioned stimulus

    (E) conditioned stimulus

83. Jay is afraid of asking women out. Rather than having Jay work his way up to asking someone out by learning to relax when thinking about doing it, his therapist goes with Jay to a bar and tells him to just go ahead and ask someone out. Which therapeutic technique is this therapist using?

    (A) A token economy

    (B) Systematic desensitization

    (C) Flooding

    (D) Free association

    (E) Aversion therapy

84. Marvin has been depressed for years. A cognitive therapist would be likely to

    (A) have Marvin develop a relaxation hierarchy

    (B) encourage Marvin to take credit for successes and downplay his failures

    (C) have Marvin talk about his father

    (D) use counter-conditioning to treat Marvin

    (E) reward Marvin for behaving in upbeat ways

85. Operant conditioning principles are the basis of

    (A) token economies

    (B) relaxation hierarchies

    (C) systematic desensitization

    (D) flooding

    (E) client-centered therapy

86. All of the following are true of Valium EXCEPT:

    (A) It is less likely than barbiturates to present the danger of addiction.

    (B) It can eliminate the effects of fear.

    (C) It is effective in calming anxiety.

    (D) It is often used to treat schizophrenia.

    (E) It is meant only for short- or medium-term use.

87. Karen believes that her boyfriend was late getting to her house because traffic is usually bad at that time of the day. Karen's explanation of her boyfriend's behavior is an example of

    (A) a situational attribution

    (B) in-group bias

    (C) a dispositional attribution

    (D) the bystander effect.

    (E) scapegoating.

88. We have a tendency to explain our own behavior and that of others in divergent ways. Which of the following terms, respectively, best illustrates how this contrast is drawn?

    (A) normative influences .. informational influences

    (B) constraints imposed by others .. situational factors

    (C) situational factors .. their own personal dispositions

    (D) personal dispositions .. situational factors

    (E) personal traits .. social roles

89. In Zimbardo's famous Stanford Prison Study, college students were randomly assigned to be either prisoners or guards. The results of this study illustrate best the effects of

    (A) mere exposure on liking

    (B) frustration on aggression

    (C) the presence of others on the successful performance of a task

    (D) the fundamental attribution error on decision making

    (E) role-playing on attitudes

90. Feelings of cognitive dissonance are likely to be highest when we perform a behavior freely and have an attitude that is

    (A) inconsistent with the behavior

    (B) consistent with the behavior

    (C) favorable toward the behavior

(D) unfavorable toward the behavior

(E) neither favorable nor unfavorable toward the behavior

91. Jeff is part of a 10-member committee appointed to hire a new secretary for his work unit. He disagrees with the other committee members about the qualifications of Candidate A and doesn't want to hire him. Jeff is most likely to go along with the others anyway if

(A) he stated his opinion publicly early in the discussion

(B) his level of self-esteem is relatively high

(C) voting is done by secret ballot

(D) the other committee members all agree with each other

(E) he feels strongly about hiring a secretary with the credentials he's seeking

92. In Milgram's studies of obedience, "teachers" delivered the highest levels of shocks to the "learner" when

(A) the two were in the same room together

(B) the experimenter called instructions in over the phone

(C) another subject refused to deliver shocks

(D) the experiment appeared to be supported by a prestigious institution

(E) the "teachers" had to hold the "learner's" hand on the shock plate

93. Students who thought they were pulling on a rope with three other people didn't pull as hard as they did when they thought they were pulling alone. This illustrates

(A) groupthink   (D) group polarization

(B) social loafing   (E) social facilitation

(C) the bystander effect

94. Which of the following phenomena most clearly contributes to groupthink?

    (A) The mere-exposure effect

    (B) Deindividuation

    (C) The bystander effect

    (D) Social facilitation

    (E) Group polarization

95. Cindy always sits near the same person in her math class. Despite the fact that he doesn't seem especially friendly, Cindy has started becoming fond of him. Cindy's growing feelings of liking illustrate

    (A) the mere-exposure effect

    (B) the bystander effect

    (C) social facilitation

    (D) the fundamental attribution error

    (E) the actor-observer difference

96. In an emergency, help is most likely to be forthcoming when

    (A) the potential helper is in a good mood

    (B) the victim appears to be a drunk

    (C) the observer has just flunked a test

    (D) several people are around to help

    (E) the observer is from a large city

97. A random sample of subjects is one in which

    (A) there are no personality differences among subjects

    (B) experimental differences between groups will be statistically significant

    (C) every member of the population has an equal chance of being included

    (D) subjects' characteristics match perfectly those of the populations they came from

(E) the experiment has just the right number of subjects

98. Each person who completed a 14-item personality test two months ago returned to complete it again just recently. The correlation between those two sets of scores was then computed. This procedure was used to assess

(A) construct validity

(B) face validity

(C) test-retest reliability

(D) split-half reliability

(E) criterion-related validity

99. By adding up all the scores in a distribution of scores, and then dividing by the number of scores that have been added, one can determine

(A) the standard deviation

(B) the mode

(C) the mean

(D) the statistical significance

(E) the median

100. In a correlational study, the researcher determines that the relationship between scores on an extraversion scale and a measure of how many friends people have is about +.44. If this relationship is statistically significant,

(A) it must be important

(B) it could not have happened by chance

(C) the questionnaires must be valid

(D) it's unlikely that the correlation in the population that the research sample came from is .00

(E) the correlation in the population the research sample came from must be +.44 as well

CLEP INTRODUCTORY PSYCHOLOGY
PRACTICE TEST 2

ANSWER KEY

1.	(B)	26.	(C)	51.	(E)	76.	(D)
2.	(E)	27.	(C)	52.	(E)	77.	(C)
3.	(C)	28.	(D)	53.	(C)	78.	(B)
4.	(B)	29.	(A)	54.	(C)	79.	(B)
5.	(A)	30.	(B)	55.	(D)	80.	(E)
6.	(D)	31.	(E)	56.	(A)	81.	(D)
7.	(C)	32.	(B)	57.	(E)	82.	(A)
8.	(D)	33.	(C)	58.	(D)	83.	(C)
9.	(D)	34.	(C)	59.	(C)	84.	(B)
10.	(B)	35.	(D)	60.	(A)	85.	(A)
11.	(E)	36.	(A)	61.	(C)	86.	(D)
12.	(E)	37.	(D)	62.	(E)	87.	(A)
13.	(E)	38.	(E)	63.	(B)	88.	(C)
14.	(D)	39.	(D)	64.	(A)	89.	(E)
15.	(C)	40.	(B)	65.	(D)	90.	(A)
16.	(B)	41.	(D)	66.	(B)	91.	(D)
17.	(C)	42.	(C)	67.	(D)	92.	(D)
18.	(A)	43.	(E)	68.	(A)	93.	(B)
19.	(B)	44.	(A)	69.	(B)	94.	(E)
20.	(E)	45.	(A)	70.	(C)	95.	(A)
21.	(D)	46.	(A)	71.	(E)	96.	(A)
22.	(B)	47.	(D)	72.	(D)	97.	(C)
23.	(A)	48.	(C)	73.	(E)	98.	(C)
24.	(C)	49.	(E)	74.	(A)	99.	(C)
25.	(E)	50.	(C)	75.	(A)	100.	(D)

DETAILED EXPLANATIONS OF ANSWERS

PRACTICE TEST 2

1. **(B)** Functionalists focus on the value that behaviors and other psychological characteristics have for an organism's adaptation to its environment. Structuralists focus on what those behaviors and characteristics are, and on finding their basic components.

2. **(E)** Behaviorists argue that it isn't necessary to know about internal mental processes to understand and predict behavior; humanists focus on studying characteristics of the self and their organization; psychoanalysts emphasize internal sources of tension and conflict; structuralists use introspection to study internal mental processes; and functionalists aren't directly concerned with the importance of internal vs. external factors in behavior, but nevertheless were interested in studying the mind.

3. **(C)** The cognitive approach is about how people think; the biological approach is about how chemistry and physiology influence behavior; humanists and psychoanalysts are interested in what people think about, but not in how thinking happens.

4. **(B)** In each of the other research methods, subjects know that their behavior is being observed.

5. **(A)** Naturalistic observation precludes asking questions, so only overt behavior can be studied. Surveys, correlational studies, and experiments necessarily involve many subjects.

6. **(D)** Experiments test cause-and-effect relationships by manipulating an independent variable (the presumed cause; in this case the presence or absence of music) and measuring the effect on the dependent variable.

7. **(C)** Hypotheses (testable predictions) are often derived from the principles of a theory, but don't in themselves organize or explain; experiments test theories; theories may make assumptions, but those assumptions aren't themselves principles; and operational definitions simply define the method used to measure a variable.

8. **(D)** People selected at random are expected to differ, the important thing is that they differ only by chance. Volunteers select themselves, and so aren't randomly chosen. An experimenter can determine how many people to select at random.

9. **(D)** The parasympathetic nervous system tends to reduce signs of arousal associated with the "fight or flight" response produced by the sympathetic nervous system.

10. **(B)** The temporal lobes are involved in hearing, the parietal lobes in the sense of touch, and the frontal lobes in organizing behavior and predicting its consequences. Association areas are located in each lobe and don't appear to play specific functions.

11. **(E)** Secretions from the pituitary gland influence the release of hormones from other glands in the endocrine system.

12. **(E)** This refers to the electrical charge inside the neuron, relative to the charge outside; the charge is positive outside and negative inside. When part of a neuron fires, that part is "depolarized."

13. **(E)** Dendrites receive signals from other cells.

14. **(D)** Broca's area is responsible for directing the muscle movements involved in speaking. Wernicke's area, another brain structure involved in speech, is the part of the brain where acoustical codes—including spoken words—are decoded and interpreted.

15. **(C)** Glia cells act as a sort of "neuronal glue," holding neurons together. They also provide myelin sheathing and nutrients, and clean up excess ions and neurotransmitters. Serotonin and dopamine are neurotransmitters that help neurons communicate with one another. Hormones affect body tissues.

16. **(B)** Acetylcholine contributes to learning and memory; dopamine influences emotions, memory, and movement; norepinephrine helps regulate arousal; and serotonin helps to regulate mood.

17. **(C)**   The corpus callosum is a bundle of nerve fibers that connects the two hemispheres of the brain. Severing it prevents seizures from spreading across the brain from one hemisphere to the other.

18. **(A)**   Perception involves selecting stimuli to attend to, organizing sensations, and interpreting what is sensed. Sensation involves detecting and encoding energy coming from stimuli.

19. **(B)**   The just-noticeable difference (or difference threshold) is the smallest difference a person can detect between two stimuli. Feature detection has to do with specific neuron's abilities to detect particular features of a stimulus (e.g., lines or angles).

20. **(E)**   Transduction involves transforming one form of energy (such as light waves or sound waves) into another form of energy (such as nerve impulses).

21. **(D)**   The iris regulates the size of the pupil and, so, how much light can enter the eye. The optic nerve carries signals from the eye to the brain; the retina is the light-sensitive surface of the inner eye; the lens is between the pupil and the retina and focuses light on the retina. The cochlea is a part of the ear.

22. **(B)**   An object that can be perceived is the "figure" and its surroundings are the "ground." Shape constancy is the ability to recognize an object when seeing it from a new angle; the phi phenomenon is the appearance of one light moving when a series of lights are turned on, then off, in succession; a perceptual set is a predisposition to interpret stimuli in a particular way; and sensation involves merely detecting stimuli, not recognizing the meaning of their patterns.

23. **(A)**   Continuity and closure are two principles of perception that illustrate the idea that people will tend to see a whole figure when there are only parts (i.e., that "the whole is greater than the sum of its parts").

24. **(C)**   The brain can detect the angle at which eyes must turn inward to view an object and use that to calculate how far away the object is. Size constancy refers to the ability to recognize an object as the same at different distances (rather than being a different, smaller object when farther away); interposition has to do with using the blocking of one object by another as a cue to relative distance; closure is the tendency to see parts as forming a whole; and motion parallax refers to the apparent backward movement of objects that are closer than a fixation point.

25. **(E)** Perceptual sets are predispositions to respond to stimuli in a particular way (such as attributing characteristics to someone because he or she belong to a particular category of people).

26. **(C)** "Circadian" is from the Latin for "about" (i.e., circa) and "day" (i.e., dies), so it means "about the day," or a 24-hour period. If a rise in body temperature happens on a daily basis, then, it reflects a circadian rhythm.

27. **(C)** Hypnogogic sensations are most likely to happen during Stage 1 sleep, the first five minutes or so of light sleep, just as one has fallen asleep.

28. **(D)** These bursts of brain activity occur during Stage 2 sleep.

29. **(A)** Narcolepsy involves unpredictable and uncontrollable attacks of sleep; insomnia involves an inability to fall asleep; REM rebound is an increase in REM sleep following a period of REM deprivation.

30. **(B)** Barbiturates and opiates (e.g., heroin and morphine) are derivatives of opium; they depress the nervous system, but they're highly addictive and have strong side-effects; amphetamines speed up the body's functions; hallucinogens (like LSD) produce distorted perceptions; and anti-psychotics treat psychological disorders that involve hallucinations or delusions, like schizophrenia.

31. **(E)** LSD causes produces hallucinations and sensory images in the absence of any appropriate sensory input.

32. **(B)** In non-associative learning, changes in responses to a stimulus happen because of exposure to that one stimulus. Habituation is a decrease in response due to repeated exposure to a stimulus. In associative learning, changes in responses happen because of relationships between stimuli (classical conditioning) or between a stimulus and a response (operant conditioning).

33. **(C)** "Conditioning" is another word for learning, so "unconditioned" responses are built-in, reflexive, unlearned behaviors.

34. **(C)** "Conditioned" (i.e., "learned") stimuli are stimuli that produce responses they didn't produce before (i.e., before being paired with an unconditioned stimulus). Dogs don't reflexively drool when they hear a bell, so salivating in response to a bell must have been learned.

35. **(D)**   Generalization is the tendency to respond to stimuli that are similar to those used during conditioning.

36. **(A)**   Generalization is the tendency to respond to stimuli that are similar to those used during conditioning; discrimination is learning not to respond to stimuli used during conditioning (so, the more a learned response generalizes, the less discrimination has taken place, and vice versa); the overjustification effect is the tendency to reduce responding, after reinforcement ends, to below the level is was at prior to being reinforced at all; operant conditioning involves rewards and punishments.

37. **(D)**   In operant conditioning terms, consequences that increase the chance of the target behavior occurring are called "reinforcement" and those that decrease the chance of target behavior occurring are called "punishment." Those that involve the loss of a stimulus are called "negative" and those involving the presentation of a stimulus are called "positive."

38. **(E)**   The overjustification effect is the tendency to reduce responding, after reinforcement ends, to below the level it was at prior to being reinforced at all (i.e., to below its "baseline" level). In Nicki's case, the baseline level of piano playing was 3 hours a week and the level she played at while being reinforced was 10 hours a week. After reinforcement ended, her piano playing dropped below the baseline level.

39. **(D)**   The councilman's behavior (visiting voters) gets reinforced only after a period of time has gone by and won't (apparently) get reinforced during that period. Thus this is an interval schedule. Because the interval is constant, it's also a fixed interval schedule.

40. **(B)**   Discrimination involves learning to respond to one stimulus and not another. In the case of operant conditioning, that happens when a (voluntary) response gets reinforced in the presence of one stimulus (e.g., a class dealing with history) but not in the presence of another (e.g., a class dealing with political science).

41. **(D)**   Shaping is also called the "method of successive approximations" and is used to create a behavior that would not ordinarily occur spontaneously and so could rarely get reinforced (and would take a long time to increase in frequency).

42. **(C)**   The availability heuristic involves using the memorability or salience of an event as the basis for judging how often it happens; the

representativeness heuristic involves using the similarity between an event and some class of events as the basis for deciding whether that event is a member of the class; confirmation bias is the tendency to look for information that confirms, rather than disconfirms, our beliefs; and belief perseverance is the tendency to maintain discredited beliefs.

43. **(E)** The availability heuristic involves using the memorability or salience of an event as the basis for judging how often it happens. The representativeness heuristic involves using the similarity between an event and some class of events as the basis for deciding whether that event is a member of the class; overconfidence refers to people's tendency to be more confident of judgments than they rationally ought to be; confirmation bias is the tendency to look for information that confirms, rather than disconfirms, our beliefs; and the framing effect refers to the tendency for people's judgments to be influenced by the way in which a problem is presented.

44. **(A)** Syntax refers to the rules for combining words in meaningful ways; pragmatics is about the ways in which people use language (e.g., sarcasm, metaphors); phonetics has to do with the perception and production of speech sounds; and telegraphic speech is the use of one- or two-word utterances in conjunction with gestures and expressions to stand for relatively complex ideas.

45. **(A)** The one-word stage begins at around 12 months; the two-word stage at around 18 months; and the multiple-word stage (there doesn't appear to be a three-word stage) at around 2 years.

46. **(A)** The term "chunking" refers to the grouping of material into manageable, and memorable, units. Rehearsal involves repeating material in order to learn it; automatic processing refers to the mental activities involved in learning things without effort; flashbulb memories are vivid memories of emotionally charged events; and the serial-position effect is the tendency for people to remember material from the middle of a list less well than material from the beginning or end of the list.

47. **(D)** The tendency for people to remember material from the beginning or end of a list better than material from the middle of a list is called the serial-position effect.

48. **(C)** Personality tests measure differences in levels of a trait; achievement tests measure learned skills or knowledge; standardized tests are tests for which scores have been obtained from large numbers of

people in order that comparisons can be made between an individual's score and those of people who share his or her characteristics in some way (e.g., same age or sex); and intelligence tests measure broadly defined problem-solving skills.

49. **(E)**   Validity has to do with whether a test measures what it's supposed to; reliability has to do with whether a test measures something consistently; correlational studies are about groups, not individuals; and factor analysis is a statistical tool used for identifying patterns in data.

50. **(C)**   According to drive-reduction theories, needs like thirst and hunger disrupt a steady internal state (i.e., homeostasis) and create a "drive" to return the body to homeostasis.

51. **(E)**   Intelligence has not been shown to affect affiliation. All the other factors have been experimentally manipulated in the lab, and have been shown to affect the desire to affiliate. Similarity of co-affiliators and the degree of possible verbal communication have also been shown to affect affiliation.

52. **(E)**   According to arousal theory, people will work to maintain an optimum level of arousal. When their arousal is low, then, they would do something to increase arousal (like jumping out of a plane).

53. **(C)**   From bottom to top, Maslow's hierarchy describes needs for nourishment, safety, belongingness and love, esteem, and self-actualization.

54. **(C)**   Cannon-Bard is not inconsistent with the idea of emotions being innate or learned; none of these theories of emotions says that emotion generates arousal; the labeling of arousal is central to Schacter's two-factor theory; the idea that arousal precedes emotional experience is central to the James-Lange theory.

55. **(D)**   According to two-factor theory, the quality of arousal is the same regardless of the emotion we experience. How we label that arousal, though, determines the quality of the emotional experience.

56. **(A)**   Performance on easy, well-learned tasks is facilitated by arousal; performance on complex, difficult tasks is made worse by arousal.

57. **(E)**   "Catharsis" is a sudden release of energy. From a psychoanalytic perspective, it takes an investment of energy to prevent oneself from expressing anger; therefore, doing something aggressive would release that energy because it's no longer needed for restraining oneself.

58. **(D)** "Nature" has to do with genetics and wired-in behavioral tendencies. "Nurture" has to do with the influence of factors outside the individual, such as upbringing, drugs, education, and so forth.

59. **(C)** Egocentricity refers to the tendency (which presumably gets weaker with age) to believe that other people think and feel what one thinks and feels oneself; in other words, a difficulty distinguishing oneself from others.

60. **(A)** One's sense of being male or female is a "gender identity;" "sexual orientation" refers to the sex toward which one is sexually attracted; biological sex is simply "sex" ("gender" refers to cultural norms of masculinity and femininity); the learning of gender is called "gender typing."

61. **(C)** Recognizing that changes (or differences) in appearance are often irrelevant to quantitative measures of objects (like their mass, volume, number, etc.) is called conservation.

62. **(E)** Authoritative parents set rules and enforce them, but are also flexible and responsive; authoritarian parents demand obedience; disengaged parents are largely unaware of what their children are up to; and permissive parents don't make many demands on their children.

63. **(B)** According to Erikson, young adults face a crisis between achieving intimacy and being left isolated.

64. **(A)** According to Kohlberg, people in the conventional stage of morality decide what to do on the basis of social approval. People in the pre-conventional stage base moral decisions on avoiding punishment or getting concrete rewards; people in the post-conventional stage make decisions based on universal rights and ethical principles.

65. **(D)** Studies that involve a group of subjects of the same age followed over a period of time are longitudinal. Cross-sectional studies involve people of different ages studied at a single point in time, and cross-sequential (sometimes called cross-lagged) studies follow people of different ages (as in a cross-sectional study) over a period of time (as in a longitudinal study). An experiment would require that an independent variable be manipulated.

66. **(B)** The term "crystallized intelligence" refers to the body of information that one has accumulated over one's life. Crytallized intelligence increases with age, whereas fluid intelligence tends to decline in late adulthood.

67. **(D)** Sex and aggression reflect the "life" and "death" instincts, respectively. The other options refer to humanistic concepts.

68. **(A)** In a reaction formation, one behaves in a manner opposite of the way in which one truly wants to behave (in order not to do something—the thing one really wants to do—that would cause anxiety). Projection involves attributing characteristics you don't like in yourself to other people; regression is the return to infantile behavior; identification involves becoming like someone else; and rationalization involves attempts to justify irrational behavior with rational arguments.

69. **(B)** Individuals fixated at the anal phase are rebellious and disdainful of authority. Thus they're either extremely neat and tidy (a reaction formation) or messy and willful.

70. **(C)** As part of a self-serving bias, people appear to view themselves favorably in comparison to others, take more credit for successes than failures, and feel overly optimistic about their futures.

71. **(E)** "Locus of control" has to do with what one sees as responsible for events in one's life. Having an internal locus of control means you see yourself as responsible for what happens to you; having an external locus of control means you see others (or uncontrollable events) as responsible for what happens to you.

72. **(D)** The trait approach emphasizes describing behavior in terms of individual differences in the levels of various traits people might have.

73. **(E)** Wendy appears to be expressing anger in a passive way, and doing it consistently over time: her husband is forced to do things he shouldn't have to do (because Wendy said she'd do them), but Wendy won't take responsibility for her role in his having to do it.

74. **(A)** Bi-polar disorder involves shifts between severely depressed moods and manic, flighty, highly active behavior accompanied by a high degree of optimism.

75. **(A)** Paranoid schizophrenics tend to have delusions of grandeur ("I'm Queen Victoria") or persecution ("the CIA is looking for me").

76. **(D)** Hallucination is a false sensation—seeing, feeling, tasting, smelling, or hearing something that isn't really there. Phobias are intense, irrational fears; neurotic behavior doesn't involve losing one's grasp on reality (hallucinations would be psychotic—a loss of contact with reality); conversion disorders involve the "conversion" of a psychological conflict into a physical symptom; and delusions are false thoughts.

77. **(C)** An inflated sense of importance is characteristic of a narcissistic personality disorder; a lack of remorse characterizes anti-social personalities; delusions of grandeur are common among paranoid schizophrenics; and theatrical, overly dramatic emotional displays characterize a histrionic personality disorder.

78. **(B)** A dysthymic disorder is somewhere between the blues and a major depression. A conversion reaction involves the physical expression of a psychological conflict; paranoid delusions are beliefs that one is being targeted by others in some way; dissociative disorders involve the fragmentation of personality; and obsessive-compulsive disorder is an anxiety disorder involving repetitive patterns of thoughts or behaviors.

79. **(B)** Phobias are a type of anxiety disorder in which the anxiety has a specific source. It would be an hallucination if the object didn't really exist; compulsions involve repetitive behaviors; and compulsions involve repetitive thoughts.

80. **(E)** When problem behaviors are thought of as symptoms of an underlying conflict that the client doesn't want to face, then obvious attempts to avoid dealing with the conflict can be interpreted as resistance. From the psychoanalytic perspective, "insight" refers to the recognition of the relationship between current behavior and past behavior, and would produce "catharsis," a release of energy that's no longer needed for repressing the conflict; a reaction formation involves expressing the opposite of what one wants to express (in this case, Kim might not only stay, she'd talk about how much she loves her mother); and free association is aimed at getting access to the repressed conflict (not avoiding it, as Kim is doing).

81. **(D)** Psychoanalysts trace problems in adults' behaviors to repressed childhood conflicts. The other therapies focus on what the client can do now to change his or her behavior.

82. **(A)** Phobic objects produce fear in a few people, but not everyone, so the fear must have been learned. In classical conditioning terms, a learned behavior is a conditioned response.

83. **(C)** Flooding involves exposing someone to an experience he/she dreads in order to force the extinction of a (learned) fear. Token economies involve rewards for desirable behavior (it's not clear that Jay will be rewarded); systematic desensitization involves experiencing a hierarchy of anxiety-producing situations from least stressful to most stressful; the psychoanalytic technique of free association involves encouraging clients to say whatever thoughts enter their minds; and aversion therapy pairs an aversive experience (such as nausea) with what would otherwise be a pleasure-producing stimulus (such as alcohol).

84. **(B)** Cognitive therapists want to change the way their clients think. Chronically depressed people are more likely than non-depressed people to blame themselves for failing and to not take credit when they succeed.

85. **(A)** In token economies, people are given tokens of some kind that have little inherent value (e.g., gold stars) and can exchange those tokens for tangible rewards (i.e., reinforcement). Thus their voluntary (i.e., operant) behavior is being reinforced. Relaxation hierarchies are used in systematic desensitization, which is based on classical conditioning principles (as is flooding). Client-centered therapy focuses on helping clients understand their "self."

86. **(D)** Valium depresses nervous system activity, and so calms people down (as do Librium and alcohol). Valium—as with benzodiazepines generally—is considered superior to barbiturates because it's less likely to become addictive, though long-term use—sometimes just a matter of weeks—can allow the body to build up tolerance.

87. **(A)** Situational attributions explain behavior in terms of something outside the actor (such as bad traffic); dispositional attributions explain behavior in terms of something about the actor's character or personality (such as not being a conscientious person).

88. **(C)** The "actor-observer difference" describes people's tendency to see themselves as influenced by situational constraints but to see others as responsible for their own behavior. That is, we're more likely to make dispositional attributions for others' behavior and situational attributions for our own.

89. **(E)**   In Zimbardo's study, people assigned to be guards quickly began to act like guards (without any direct pressure to do so). Similarly, people assigned to be prisoners began to act like prisoners.

90. **(A)**   "Dissonance" is a state of tension that stems from doing something one is opposed to doing. If the behavior can be blamed on something situational (e.g., "I got a lot of money to do that" or "I was forced to do that"), then there isn't much tension. But when we choose to do something that's inconsistent with our values, beliefs, or attitudes, we feel a great deal of tension.

91. **(D)**   Conformity is more likely when one faces a unanimous majority. Conformity is less likely after making a public commitment to a position, when one has high self-esteem, when one is anonymous, and when the issue is something one feels deeply about.

92. **(D)**   Obedience was reduced when teachers were close to the learners, when the experimenter (i.e., the authority) was at a distance, another subject modeled disobedience, and when the teachers could not distance themselves from what they were doing.

93. **(B)**   Social loafing is a reduction in effort on the part of the individual when working on a group task (relative to the effort put in when working alone). Groupthink is a desire for group harmony that produces acquiescence when making a decision; the bystander effect is the tendency for people not to give help in an emergency when other bystanders are around; group polarization is a tendency for people with similar opinions to shift their opinions in a more extreme direction after discussion; and social facilitation is an improvement in performance when in the presence of others.

94. **(E)**   Groupthink is an approach to solving problems that focuses on achieving consensus at the expense of considering fully all the relevant options. Group polarization involves a shift in a group's collective opinion toward a more extreme position. Thus, group polarization would contribute to a distortion of opinions that would encourage groupthink.

95. **(A)**   Within certain limits, as novel things or persons become more familiar, they also become more likable. The more we see someone, the more likely we are to like him/her.

96. **(A)**   One of the most robust findings in psychology is that happy people are helpful people. People are less likely to be helpful, though,

when they see the victim as responsible for his or her own misfortune, when they're in a bad mood, when others could take responsibility for helping, and when they live in a metropolitan area.

97. **(C)**   Random sampling doesn't guarantee that groups of subjects, or the subjects within those groups, won't differ from one another just by chance, so personality differences within a group are likely, there will probably be some chance difference between two randomly selected groups, and subjects in a sample are likely to differ to some extent from the population those subjects came from (just by chance). Also, any number of subjects can be randomly sampled—that's determined by the experimenter, not by chance.

98. **(C)**   In this case, an entire test was completed twice (hence "test-retest") as a way to determine the consistency of subjects' ratings (i.e., the test's reliability).

99. **(C)**   The standard deviation is a measure of how widely dispersed scores are around the distribution's mean; the mode is the most commonly occurring score in the distribution; the median is the score below which half of all scores in the distribution fall. Statistical significance is an estimate of the likelihood that the results of a study happened by chance.

100. **(D)**   Statistically significant effects can be trivial and could happen by chance (in fact, by definition, they could happen 5% of the time by chance). Statistical significance tells you nothing about the adequacy of the measures used in a study. Statistical significance only tells you if the correlation in the population is likely to differ from zero, not what that correlation actually is.

ANSWER SHEETS

CLEP INTRODUCTORY PSYCHOLOGY

TEST 1

1. Ⓐ Ⓑ Ⓒ Ⓓ Ⓔ	34. Ⓐ Ⓑ Ⓒ Ⓓ Ⓔ	67. Ⓐ Ⓑ Ⓒ Ⓓ Ⓔ
2. Ⓐ Ⓑ Ⓒ Ⓓ Ⓔ	35. Ⓐ Ⓑ Ⓒ Ⓓ Ⓔ	68. Ⓐ Ⓑ Ⓒ Ⓓ Ⓔ
3. Ⓐ Ⓑ Ⓒ Ⓓ Ⓔ	36. Ⓐ Ⓑ Ⓒ Ⓓ Ⓔ	69. Ⓐ Ⓑ Ⓒ Ⓓ Ⓔ
4. Ⓐ Ⓑ Ⓒ Ⓓ Ⓔ	37. Ⓐ Ⓑ Ⓒ Ⓓ Ⓔ	70. Ⓐ Ⓑ Ⓒ Ⓓ Ⓔ
5. Ⓐ Ⓑ Ⓒ Ⓓ Ⓔ	38. Ⓐ Ⓑ Ⓒ Ⓓ Ⓔ	71. Ⓐ Ⓑ Ⓒ Ⓓ Ⓔ
6. Ⓐ Ⓑ Ⓒ Ⓓ Ⓔ	39. Ⓐ Ⓑ Ⓒ Ⓓ Ⓔ	72. Ⓐ Ⓑ Ⓒ Ⓓ Ⓔ
7. Ⓐ Ⓑ Ⓒ Ⓓ Ⓔ	40. Ⓐ Ⓑ Ⓒ Ⓓ Ⓔ	73. Ⓐ Ⓑ Ⓒ Ⓓ Ⓔ
8. Ⓐ Ⓑ Ⓒ Ⓓ Ⓔ	41. Ⓐ Ⓑ Ⓒ Ⓓ Ⓔ	74. Ⓐ Ⓑ Ⓒ Ⓓ Ⓔ
9. Ⓐ Ⓑ Ⓒ Ⓓ Ⓔ	42. Ⓐ Ⓑ Ⓒ Ⓓ Ⓔ	75. Ⓐ Ⓑ Ⓒ Ⓓ Ⓔ
10. Ⓐ Ⓑ Ⓒ Ⓓ Ⓔ	43. Ⓐ Ⓑ Ⓒ Ⓓ Ⓔ	76. Ⓐ Ⓑ Ⓒ Ⓓ Ⓔ
11. Ⓐ Ⓑ Ⓒ Ⓓ Ⓔ	44. Ⓐ Ⓑ Ⓒ Ⓓ Ⓔ	77. Ⓐ Ⓑ Ⓒ Ⓓ Ⓔ
12. Ⓐ Ⓑ Ⓒ Ⓓ Ⓔ	45. Ⓐ Ⓑ Ⓒ Ⓓ Ⓔ	78. Ⓐ Ⓑ Ⓒ Ⓓ Ⓔ
13. Ⓐ Ⓑ Ⓒ Ⓓ Ⓔ	46. Ⓐ Ⓑ Ⓒ Ⓓ Ⓔ	79. Ⓐ Ⓑ Ⓒ Ⓓ Ⓔ
14. Ⓐ Ⓑ Ⓒ Ⓓ Ⓔ	47. Ⓐ Ⓑ Ⓒ Ⓓ Ⓔ	80. Ⓐ Ⓑ Ⓒ Ⓓ Ⓔ
15. Ⓐ Ⓑ Ⓒ Ⓓ Ⓔ	48. Ⓐ Ⓑ Ⓒ Ⓓ Ⓔ	81. Ⓐ Ⓑ Ⓒ Ⓓ Ⓔ
16. Ⓐ Ⓑ Ⓒ Ⓓ Ⓔ	49. Ⓐ Ⓑ Ⓒ Ⓓ Ⓔ	82. Ⓐ Ⓑ Ⓒ Ⓓ Ⓔ
17. Ⓐ Ⓑ Ⓒ Ⓓ Ⓔ	50. Ⓐ Ⓑ Ⓒ Ⓓ Ⓔ	83. Ⓐ Ⓑ Ⓒ Ⓓ Ⓔ
18. Ⓐ Ⓑ Ⓒ Ⓓ Ⓔ	51. Ⓐ Ⓑ Ⓒ Ⓓ Ⓔ	84. Ⓐ Ⓑ Ⓒ Ⓓ Ⓔ
19. Ⓐ Ⓑ Ⓒ Ⓓ Ⓔ	52. Ⓐ Ⓑ Ⓒ Ⓓ Ⓔ	85. Ⓐ Ⓑ Ⓒ Ⓓ Ⓔ
20. Ⓐ Ⓑ Ⓒ Ⓓ Ⓔ	53. Ⓐ Ⓑ Ⓒ Ⓓ Ⓔ	86. Ⓐ Ⓑ Ⓒ Ⓓ Ⓔ
21. Ⓐ Ⓑ Ⓒ Ⓓ Ⓔ	54. Ⓐ Ⓑ Ⓒ Ⓓ Ⓔ	87. Ⓐ Ⓑ Ⓒ Ⓓ Ⓔ
22. Ⓐ Ⓑ Ⓒ Ⓓ Ⓔ	55. Ⓐ Ⓑ Ⓒ Ⓓ Ⓔ	88. Ⓐ Ⓑ Ⓒ Ⓓ Ⓔ
23. Ⓐ Ⓑ Ⓒ Ⓓ Ⓔ	56. Ⓐ Ⓑ Ⓒ Ⓓ Ⓔ	89. Ⓐ Ⓑ Ⓒ Ⓓ Ⓔ
24. Ⓐ Ⓑ Ⓒ Ⓓ Ⓔ	57. Ⓐ Ⓑ Ⓒ Ⓓ Ⓔ	90. Ⓐ Ⓑ Ⓒ Ⓓ Ⓔ
25. Ⓐ Ⓑ Ⓒ Ⓓ Ⓔ	58. Ⓐ Ⓑ Ⓒ Ⓓ Ⓔ	91. Ⓐ Ⓑ Ⓒ Ⓓ Ⓔ
26. Ⓐ Ⓑ Ⓒ Ⓓ Ⓔ	59. Ⓐ Ⓑ Ⓒ Ⓓ Ⓔ	92. Ⓐ Ⓑ Ⓒ Ⓓ Ⓔ
27. Ⓐ Ⓑ Ⓒ Ⓓ Ⓔ	60. Ⓐ Ⓑ Ⓒ Ⓓ Ⓔ	93. Ⓐ Ⓑ Ⓒ Ⓓ Ⓔ
28. Ⓐ Ⓑ Ⓒ Ⓓ Ⓔ	61. Ⓐ Ⓑ Ⓒ Ⓓ Ⓔ	94. Ⓐ Ⓑ Ⓒ Ⓓ Ⓔ
29. Ⓐ Ⓑ Ⓒ Ⓓ Ⓔ	62. Ⓐ Ⓑ Ⓒ Ⓓ Ⓔ	95. Ⓐ Ⓑ Ⓒ Ⓓ Ⓔ
30. Ⓐ Ⓑ Ⓒ Ⓓ Ⓔ	63. Ⓐ Ⓑ Ⓒ Ⓓ Ⓔ	96. Ⓐ Ⓑ Ⓒ Ⓓ Ⓔ
31. Ⓐ Ⓑ Ⓒ Ⓓ Ⓔ	64. Ⓐ Ⓑ Ⓒ Ⓓ Ⓔ	97. Ⓐ Ⓑ Ⓒ Ⓓ Ⓔ
32. Ⓐ Ⓑ Ⓒ Ⓓ Ⓔ	65. Ⓐ Ⓑ Ⓒ Ⓓ Ⓔ	98. Ⓐ Ⓑ Ⓒ Ⓓ Ⓔ
33. Ⓐ Ⓑ Ⓒ Ⓓ Ⓔ	66. Ⓐ Ⓑ Ⓒ Ⓓ Ⓔ	99. Ⓐ Ⓑ Ⓒ Ⓓ Ⓔ
		100. Ⓐ Ⓑ Ⓒ Ⓓ Ⓔ

CLEP INTRODUCTORY PSYCHOLOGY

TEST 2

1. (A) (B) (C) (D) (E)
2. (A) (B) (C) (D) (E)
3. (A) (B) (C) (D) (E)
4. (A) (B) (C) (D) (E)
5. (A) (B) (C) (D) (E)
6. (A) (B) (C) (D) (E)
7. (A) (B) (C) (D) (E)
8. (A) (B) (C) (D) (E)
9. (A) (B) (C) (D) (E)
10. (A) (B) (C) (D) (E)
11. (A) (B) (C) (D) (E)
12. (A) (B) (C) (D) (E)
13. (A) (B) (C) (D) (E)
14. (A) (B) (C) (D) (E)
15. (A) (B) (C) (D) (E)
16. (A) (B) (C) (D) (E)
17. (A) (B) (C) (D) (E)
18. (A) (B) (C) (D) (E)
19. (A) (B) (C) (D) (E)
20. (A) (B) (C) (D) (E)
21. (A) (B) (C) (D) (E)
22. (A) (B) (C) (D) (E)
23. (A) (B) (C) (D) (E)
24. (A) (B) (C) (D) (E)
25. (A) (B) (C) (D) (E)
26. (A) (B) (C) (D) (E)
27. (A) (B) (C) (D) (E)
28. (A) (B) (C) (D) (E)
29. (A) (B) (C) (D) (E)
30. (A) (B) (C) (D) (E)
31. (A) (B) (C) (D) (E)
32. (A) (B) (C) (D) (E)
33. (A) (B) (C) (D) (E)

34. (A) (B) (C) (D) (E)
35. (A) (B) (C) (D) (E)
36. (A) (B) (C) (D) (E)
37. (A) (B) (C) (D) (E)
38. (A) (B) (C) (D) (E)
39. (A) (B) (C) (D) (E)
40. (A) (B) (C) (D) (E)
41. (A) (B) (C) (D) (E)
42. (A) (B) (C) (D) (E)
43. (A) (B) (C) (D) (E)
44. (A) (B) (C) (D) (E)
45. (A) (B) (C) (D) (E)
46. (A) (B) (C) (D) (E)
47. (A) (B) (C) (D) (E)
48. (A) (B) (C) (D) (E)
49. (A) (B) (C) (D) (E)
50. (A) (B) (C) (D) (E)
51. (A) (B) (C) (D) (E)
52. (A) (B) (C) (D) (E)
53. (A) (B) (C) (D) (E)
54. (A) (B) (C) (D) (E)
55. (A) (B) (C) (D) (E)
56. (A) (B) (C) (D) (E)
57. (A) (B) (C) (D) (E)
58. (A) (B) (C) (D) (E)
59. (A) (B) (C) (D) (E)
60. (A) (B) (C) (D) (E)
61. (A) (B) (C) (D) (E)
62. (A) (B) (C) (D) (E)
63. (A) (B) (C) (D) (E)
64. (A) (B) (C) (D) (E)
65. (A) (B) (C) (D) (E)
66. (A) (B) (C) (D) (E)

67. (A) (B) (C) (D) (E)
68. (A) (B) (C) (D) (E)
69. (A) (B) (C) (D) (E)
70. (A) (B) (C) (D) (E)
71. (A) (B) (C) (D) (E)
72. (A) (B) (C) (D) (E)
73. (A) (B) (C) (D) (E)
74. (A) (B) (C) (D) (E)
75. (A) (B) (C) (D) (E)
76. (A) (B) (C) (D) (E)
77. (A) (B) (C) (D) (E)
78. (A) (B) (C) (D) (E)
79. (A) (B) (C) (D) (E)
80. (A) (B) (C) (D) (E)
81. (A) (B) (C) (D) (E)
82. (A) (B) (C) (D) (E)
83. (A) (B) (C) (D) (E)
84. (A) (B) (C) (D) (E)
85. (A) (B) (C) (D) (E)
86. (A) (B) (C) (D) (E)
87. (A) (B) (C) (D) (E)
88. (A) (B) (C) (D) (E)
89. (A) (B) (C) (D) (E)
90. (A) (B) (C) (D) (E)
91. (A) (B) (C) (D) (E)
92. (A) (B) (C) (D) (E)
93. (A) (B) (C) (D) (E)
94. (A) (B) (C) (D) (E)
95. (A) (B) (C) (D) (E)
96. (A) (B) (C) (D) (E)
97. (A) (B) (C) (D) (E)
98. (A) (B) (C) (D) (E)
99. (A) (B) (C) (D) (E)
100. (A) (B) (C) (D) (E)

Glossary

Absolute refractory period – A brief period toward the end of neural stimulation during which the nerve cannot be restimulated.

Absolute threshold – The lowest level of intensity of a stimulus at which its presence or absence can be correctly detected 50 percent of the time.

Accommodation – In Piaget's system, the adaptive modification of the child's cognitive structures in order to deal with new objects or experiences. (See Assimilation.)

ACTH (adrenocorticotrophic hormone) – A hormone secreted by the pituitary gland in response to stress, causing the adrenal cortex to secrete corticosterone.

Action potential – The nerve impulse; the changes in electrical potential along a nerve fiber that constitute the nerve impulse as it travels through the axon.

Adrenaline – Also called epinephrine; a substance produced by the adrenal gland which is related to increases in general arousal.

Afferent nerves – Nerves carried by the dorsal root which relay sensory impulses (information about the environment) to the central nervous system; sometimes used synonymously with sensory nerves.

Algorithm – A method for attacking a problem which is assured of success; often involves repetitive operations which survey the possibilities at each step.

All-or-none law – The principle that the axon of a neuron fires either with full strength or not at all to a stimulus, regardless of its intensity, provided the stimulus is at least at the threshold value.

Amygdala – A part of the limbic system, the system where emotion is organized, it is located between the hypothalamus and pituitary gland and becomes active whenever we encounter anything new or unexpected.

Androgens – Substances associated with male sex hormone activity in vertebrates, produced mainly by the testes and to a small extent by ovaries and the adrenal cortex.

Aphasia – Loss or impairment of the ability to express or receive linguistic communications, resulting from cerebral damage to the parietotemporal cortex.

Assimilation – In Piaget's theory, the taking in of new information. Assimilation ultimately results in the accommodation of a schema to the new information.

Associationism – In psychophysics and cognition the theoretical approach that complex ideas are the result of associations between simple elements. In learning

theories synonymous with the S-R connection (stimulus with response).

Autonomic nervous system (ANS) – The peripheral nervous system that controls the function of many glands and smooth-muscle organs. It is divided into the sympathetic and parasympathetic systems.

Axon – The elongated part of a nerve cell body which carries the nerve impulse away from the cell body toward another nerve fiber or neural structure.

Babinski reflex – A reflex present in the newborn child, but disappearing later in life. It involves fanning the toes as a result of being tickled in the center of the soles of the feet. Normal adults curl their toes inward rather than fanning them outward.

Behavior modification – The application of scientifically derived principles (usually from learning) to the control of human behavior. Both classical and operant conditioning may be employed.

Behaviorism – A system of psychology, founded by John B. Watson, which studied observable, measurable stimuli and responses only, without reference to consciousness or mental constructs, which the system argues have no real utility. The objective is to predict the response evoked by certain stimuli.

Binocular disparity – The minor difference between the two retinal images when viewing a solid (three-dimensional) object. It is caused by the separation of the two eyes with a consequent difference in the visual angle. Binocular disparity is important in depth perception.

Biofeedback – The use of a device to reveal physiological responses that are usually unobservable. Biofeedback experiments typically inform the subject about his heart rate, respiration rate, EEG activity, or similar responses in order to enable him to achieve some degree of control over the responses. Biofeedback is now often used in psychotherapy in teaching individuals to control their own physiological states (e.g., to reduce anxiety and its symptoms).

Broca's area – One of the areas of the cerebral cortex, located in the frontal lobe, which is important for the motor aspects of speech. Located in the inferior frontal gyrus in the left cerebral hemisphere of right-handed individuals and in the right hemisphere for left-handed people.

Cannon-Bard theory – A theory of emotion that holds that bodily reaction and emotional experience occur simultaneously because they are both controlled from the same place in the midbrain. It challenged the James-Lange theory of emotion (see James-Lange).

Catatonia – Generally, any reaction in which there is a complete withdrawal characterized by an inhibition of movement, speech, and responsiveness to the environment.

Central nervous system (CNS) – The brain and spinal cord.

Cerebral cortex – The outermost half-inch layer of the cerebral hemispheres, it contains motor, sensory, and intellectual processes. It is made up of gray tinted cells and thus is sometimes called gray matter. (Also known as the neocortex of the new brain.)

Cerebrum – The largest and most highly developed part of the nervous system in higher animals. It is divided into the right and left cerebral hemispheres which are connected to each other by the corpus callosum. It occupies the entire upper area of the cranium and is involved in the regulation of sensory processes, thought formation, and motor activity.

Chromosomes – Structures within the nucleus of a cell which contain the genes. Human cells contain 23 pairs of chromosomes for a total of 46.

Circadian rhythms – Cyclical patterns of change in physiological functions such as hunger, sleep, or body temperature occurring at approximately 24-hour intervals.

Classical conditioning – (also known as Pavlovian or Respondent or Type S conditioning) A form of learning in which an originally neutral stimulus repeatedly paired with a reinforcer elicits a response. The neutral stimulus is the conditioning stimulus (CS), the reinforcer is the unconditioned stimulus (UCS), the unlearned response is the unconditioned response (UR), and the learned response is the conditioned response (CR).

Cognitive dissonance (Festinger) – An uncomfortable psychological conflict between beliefs and behavior. Also the motivational position that the individual will take to reduce the dissonance.

Comparative psychology – The branch of psychology which compares behavioral differences among the species on the phylogenetic scale to discover developmental trends.

Compulsion – An irrational and unwanted repetition of an activity which arises when one can no longer control an anxiety or attempts to satisfy an obsession.

Concordance rate – Probability that one of a pair of twins will show a given characteristic, given that the other twin has the characteristic.

Concurrent validity – A measure of how well a test measures what it was designed to measure by comparing the test results of the experimental group with test results of those people who are already in the field for which the test was designed.

Conditioned response (CR) – In classical conditioning, the response elicited by the conditioned stimulus. It usually resembles its corresponding unconditioned response.

Conditioned stimulus (CS) – An originally neutral stimulus that, through repeated pairings with an unconditioned stimulus, becomes effective in eliciting the conditioned response.

Cones – The cone-shaped photoreceptor cells located in the retina, particularly the fovea, which are responsible for color and high-acuity vision.

Confounding – Simultaneous variation of a second variable with an independent variable of interest so that any effect on the dependent variable cannot be attributed with certainty to the independent variable; inherent in correlational research.

Congruence (Rogers) – What is experienced inside and what is expressed outwardly are consistent.

Conservation – Piaget's term implying that certain quantitative attributes of objects remain unchanged unless something is added to or taken away from them. Such characteristics of objects as mass, number, area, volume, and so forth are capable of being conserved. For example, at a certain level of development one realizes that the amount of water is not changed by pouring it into glasses of different shapes.

Construct validity – The extent to which a particular item in a test is a true measure of some abstract trait or concept that can only be verified indirectly.

Content validity – The extent to which a particular instrument samples the behavior it is supposed to measure or predict.

Control group – The group of subjects in an experiment which is statistically equivalent in all respects to the experimental group, except that it does not receive the treatment of the independent variable (the experimental treatment). Thus the control group can be used as a comparison to the experimental group to ascertain whether subjects were affected by the experimental procedure.

Convergent thinking – As termed by Guilford, thinking which results in a unique correct solution to a problem.

Conversion reaction – A neurotic reaction which reduces anxiety by inactivation of part of the body; the psychological problem is converted into a physical one which prevents anxiety-provoking behavior. The underlying psychological conflict is transformed into a sensory or motor symptom, such as blindness or paralysis.

Corpus callosum – The structure consisting of a large group of nerve fibers that connect the left and right hemispheres of the cerebrum, allowing the hemispheres to communicate with each other.

Correlation coefficient – A statistical index expressing the degree of relationship between two variables. The range of possible values is from –1 to +1. The numerical size of the correlation is an expression of the strength of the relationship. The sign of the correlation coefficient is an indication of the direction of the relationship. A positive correlation indicates that a change in one variable is associated with a change in the other variable in the same direction. A negative correlation indicates an inverse relationship between the two variables. A correlation of .00 represents no relationship between the variables.

Counterconditioning – The weakening or elimination of a conditioned response by the learning of a new response that is incompatible with, and stronger than, the one to be extinguished. It is used in therapy to replace unacceptable responses with acceptable ones.

Cross-sectional research – A research strategy that tests at a given period of time a sample of persons or variables that are representative on several dimensions of the population as a whole. Age and ability level are two frequently used variables.

Crystallized intelligence – Intelligence used in the application of already-learned materials which is usually considered to be rigid or unchanging.

Defense mechanism – As termed by Freud, the unconscious process by which an individual protects himself from anxiety. Defense mechanisms discussed by Freud include repression, rationalization, reaction formation, projection, isolation, introjection, regression, and thought dissociation. These mechanisms are often termed ego defenses.

Deindividuation – Relative anonymity of individual characteristics and identifications in certain social situations such as mobs and crowds.

Delusion – A belief or thought that a person maintains as true despite irrefutable evidence that it is false, for example, believing that one is being persecuted; this is characteristic of psychotic reactions.

Dendrite – A neural fiber that transmits electrical impulses toward the cell body of a neuron.

Denial – A defense mechanism in which there is minimization of the importance of a situation or event or of unacceptable impulses or feelings.

Dependent variable – That factor which the experimenter wants to measure, which may be affected by the independent variable.

Depolarization – The process by which the electrical charge of a neuron reverses and becomes positive during the passage of an action potential.

Diathesis-stress theory – Theory of what causes schizophrenia; states that schizophrenia develops when there is a genetic predisposition (diathesis) present and there are environmental factors (stress) that trigger the disorder.

Differential threshold (or **just noticeable difference**) – Given an initial level of stimulation, the DL is the minimally effective stimulus difference which is correctly reported by the subject as being different.

By convention a 75 percent judgment rate has been adopted.

Discrimination learning – Learning to distinguish between two or more different stimuli, or between the presence and absence of a stimulus. In general, any learning in which the task is to make choices between alternatives.

Dissociative disorders – A group of disorders involving the abandonment of the sense of self-consistency characteristic of normal functioning. Dissociative behavior is evident in sleepwalking (somnambulism), amnesia, fugue, and multiple-personality (dissociative identity disorder).

Divergent thinking – Guilford's term for the type of thinking that produces several different solutions for a problem. Divergent thinking is assumed to be closely related to creativity, and the term is often used interchangeably with it.

Double blind – An experimental technique in which neither the experimenter nor the subject knows who is in the experimental and control groups. The double-blind technique is used to control for demand characteristics and other extraneous variables.

Drive – A goal-directed tendency of an organism based on a change in organic processes; any strong stimulus that impels an organism to action. For example, the hunger drive results from the need for food.

Echoic memory – Information stored briefly as an auditory image of a stimulus.

Efferent nerves – Nerves that transmit impulses from the central nervous system to the end organs.

Egocentrism – Lack of differentiation between one's own point of view and that of others. As used by Piaget, it refers to the early adolescent's failure to differentiate between what he and others are thinking about. Young children's thinking is heavily egocentric.

Eidetic imagery – Ability to retain an image of a picture or a scene with great clarity for a fairly long period of time. Sometimes called "photographic memory."

Electroconvulsive shock (ECS) – A form of psychotherapy used in the treatment of severe depression and manic depressive psychosis. An electrical current is passed through the brain resulting in convulsions and a short period of unconsciousness. Also called electroshock therapy.

Endocrine system – The functioning order of glands which produce hormones, it is central in the control and regulation of behavior and interacts closely with the nervous system.

Equilibration – As developed by Piaget, a term referring to a balance between assimilation and accommodation. The concept of equilibration is of primary importance to Piaget's explanation of motivation. He assumed that an individual constantly interacts with his or her environment through assimilation and accommodation to achieve a state of equilibrium.

Erogenous zone – An area of the body which, when stimulated, gives rise to sexual feeling.

Ethology – The study of organisms and their behavior in their natural habitats.

Eugenics – A form of genetic engineering that selects specific individuals for reproduction. The term was coined by Galton and is really an expression of the belief that individuals should be selected for breeding purposes in order to enhance racial characteristics.

Evoked potential – A very small change in voltage recorded from the cerebral cortex of the brain following stimulation of one of the sense modalities.

Excitatory postsynaptic potential (EPSP) – Depolarizing effects of synaptic transmission on the postsynaptic neuron.

Experimental group – In a scientific experiment, those subjects who respond to an independent variable that is "specially" manipulated by the experimenter; the responses of the experimental group can then be compared with the responses of the control group.

Extinction – In classical conditioning, the gradual disappearance of the conditioned response. This occurs with repeated presentation of the conditioned stimulus in the absence of the unconditioned stimulus. In instrumental conditioning, the elimination of a learned behavior resulting from withholding all reinforcement of that behavior.

Extrinsic motivation – Motivation based on material rewards, not inherently internalized.

Fixation – (1) In psychoanalytic theory, the failure of psychosexual development to proceed normally from one stage to the next, so that an individual's libidinal energy must in part be expended to satisfy motives appropriate to an earlier stage. (2) In perception, the point at which the eyes are directed. (3) In behavior, an inability to reject an incorrect stimulus or extinguish an incorrect response for a correct response. (4) In personality, a relatively strong and enduring emotional attachment for another person.

Fixed-action pattern (FAP) – Unvarying sequences of movement, keyed by a releaser, sign, or stimulus which are species-specific.

Fluid intelligence – Intelligence that can adjust to new situations; usually considered as flexible or adaptive thinking.

Forebrain – The frontmost division of the brain, encompassing the thalamus, hypothalamus, and cerebral hemispheres. This part of the brain is responsible for "higher" cognitive processes in humans.

Formal operational period – The fourth stage of cognitive development as proposed by Piaget, it occurs during early adolescence, as the teenager learns to conceive of events beyond the present, imagine hypothetical situations, and develop a complex system of logic.

Free-floating anxiety – Anxiety reactions that have no referent in the environment.

Frequency principle – A physiological law stating that a neuron will fire more rapidly to stronger stimuli than weaker ones, generating more action potentials per given period of time.

Frustration-aggression hypothesis – A theory proposed by Dollard and Miller, according to which the only cause of aggression is frustration. Further, that frustration always leads to some kind of aggressive reaction, whether explicit or implicit.

Fugue state – A defense by actual flight; that is, a neurotic dissociative reaction in which a person has amnesia for the past, but avoids the anxiety associated with such loss of identity. This is accomplished by developing a new identity and fleeing from the intolerable situation. An individual's activities during the fugue could range from spending a great deal of time in movie theaters to starting a completely new life.

Functional fixedness – In problem solving, a tendency or mental set in which one considers only the common uses of objects, rather than the possibilities for novel or unusual functions.

Functionalism – Early school of psychological thought which emphasized how conscious behavior helps one adapt to the environment and the role learning plays in this adaptive process. This school of thought held that the mind should be studied in terms of its usefulness to the organism in adapting to its environment.

"g" factor – Spearman's construct for a hypothetical factor, presumably measured by a test of general intelligence, which affects performance on a variety of different tasks (as opposed to specific aptitudes).

Ganglion – A cluster of nerve cell bodies that can be located outside of the central nervous system or in the subcortical regions of the brain.

Gene – An area within a chromosome composed of deoxyribonucleic acid (DNA) that determines hereditary traits.

General adaptation syndrome (GAS) – A pattern of physiological responses to extreme stress including increased autonomic activity and longer-term endocrine activity.

Gestalt psychology – Founded by Max Wertheimer, the basic premise is that "the whole is greater than the sum of its parts." Gestalt psychology not only contends that stimuli are perceived as whole images rather than as parts built into images, but also maintains that the whole determines the parts instead of the parts determining the whole. The theory originally focused on perception; however, it is applicable to a broad range of areas.

Gland – A bodily structure whose function is to manufacture chemicals, called hormones, that are secreted into the bloodstream and regulate bodily activities. The two general types are endocrine glands and exocrine glands.

Graded potential – The sum of the excitation and inhibition at a given synapse; generator potential; receptor potential.

Group-centered therapy – The term applied to the system of group therapy developed by Carl Rogers and associates in which the individuals in the group rather than the therapist have the primary role in the therapeutic relationship.

Hallucination – Perception of an external object, often bizarre in nature, in the absence of stimulation.

Halo effect – The tendency, when rating an individual on one characteristic, to be influenced by another characteristic of his personality (e.g., physically attractive people are more likely to be judged as intelligent than unattractive people).

Hawthorne effect – Generally, the effect on subjects' performance attributable to their knowledge that they are serving as experimental subjects or being treated in a special manner. Sometimes, the tendency for people to work harder when experiencing a sense of participation in something new and special.

Heritability – A statistical concept which reflects the percentage of variability in a trait that is associated with differences in the genetic composition of the individuals in the group. The capability of being inherited.

Heuristic – A principle or strategy used in problem solving which serves as a device for shortening the solution process; often used when there are many different ways to solve a problem; a solution is not guaranteed.

Hierarchy of needs – A proposal (Abraham Maslow) that arranges motives in an order in which those lower in the hierarchy must be satisfied before the higher ones can be satisfied. The lower motives are considered to be food, shelter, and so on, progressing to "self-actualization" as the motive highest in the hierarchy.

Higher-order conditioning – A form of classical conditioning in which the previously trained conditioned stimulus now functions as an unconditioned stimulus to train a new conditioned stimulus.

Homeostasis – A state of optimal organismic balance, brought about by internal regulatory mechanisms.

Hormone – A chemical manufactured and secreted into the bloodstream by an endocrine gland, which may then activate another gland or help to regulate bodily functioning and behavior.

Hypnagogic imagery – Imagery that occurs as one is dropping off to sleep. It may be visual, auditory, or somesthetic, and is more vivid in some people than in others.

Hypothalamus – A group of nuclei in the forebrain that controls the involuntary functions through the autonomic nervous system. It helps to control many basic drives and emotional processes, including sleep, thirst, temperature, sex, and hunger. It also controls much of the endocrine system's activities through connections with the pituitary gland.

Hypothesis – A testable statement that offers a predicted relationship between dependent and independent variables.

Idiographic – The approach to personality study that emphasized those aspects of personality unique to each person.

Incentive motivation – An explanation for human behavior, referring to the belief that it is the reinforcing property of the outcome of behavior that determines whether or not the individual will behave. It is the incentive value of a behavioral outcome that determines its occurrence or nonoccurrence.

Independent variable – In psychological research, the condition which the psychologist manipulates. By convention, it is plotted on the Y axis.

Individual differences – Refers to the fact that all individuals vary and are different from other individuals, even though they may have some things in common.

Inhibitory postsynaptic potential (IPSP) – Hyperpolarization of the membrane of a postsynaptic neuron which decreases the probability of neural firing.

Instinct – An invariant sequence of complex behaviors that is observed in all members of a species and that is released by specific stimuli in the apparent absence of learning. Innate behaviors that are unaffected by practice.

Instrumental behavior – Activity that usually achieves some goal or satisfies a need.

Instrumental conditioning – (See Operant conditioning.)

Insulin – A hormone secreted by the islands of Langerhans in the pancreas. It is involved in the utilization of sugar and carbohydrates in the body. Also used in insulin shock therapy.

Intermittent reinforcement – Any pattern of reinforcement which is not continuous. It may vary according to ratio or interval.

Internal consistency – Degree of relationship among the items of a test, that is, the extent to which the same examinees tend to get each item right. Measures of reliability based upon a single testing are really measures of internal consistency.

Interposition – A monocular depth cue in which one object appears closer to the viewer because it partially blocks the view of another object.

Interval schedules – A reinforcement schedule in which reinforcement is delivered after a response that has been made at the end of a given time period.

Intrinsic rewards – A form of reward that results from the activity itself because the activity is interesting, pleasurable, and rewarding.

James-Lange theory of emotion – A theory proposing that emotion-producing stimuli generate physical reactions, which in turn are perceived as felt emotions.

jnd (just noticeable difference) – The smallest difference between two stimuli that can be detected reliably (by convention, 50 percent of the time).

Kinesthesis – The sense of movement and bodily position, as mediated by receptors in the muscles, tendons, and joints.

Latent learning – Learning that appears to occur in the absence of reinforcement, facilitating performance in later trials when reinforcement is introduced.

Learned helplessness – (Seligman) The acceptance of what seem to be the unalterable consequences of a situation on the basis of previous experience or information, even if change may now be possible.

Learning set – An acquired ability to learn more rapidly in new learning situations because of previously learned responses.

Libido – The name given in Freudian theory to the instinctual or id energy that is the source of all psychological energy. Sometimes used to refer specifically to sexual motivation.

Limbic system – A group of anatomical structures surrounding the brain stem; thought to be involved with motivated behavior and emotion.

Lobotomy – Type of psychosurgery that involves severing the connections between the frontal lobes and the rest of the brain. It has been used to treat extremely hyperemotional mental patients but is infrequently used today.

Locus of control – (Rotter) A personality construct which is dependent upon whether the individual perceives rewards as being contingent upon his or her own behavior.

Longitudinal study – An investigation conducted over a fairly long period of time, using the same subjects throughout; the study may be used to determine how age, the independent variable, affects behavior.

Malleus – The outer of the three bones in the middle ear that transmit vibrations from the eardrum to the cochlea. Sometimes referred to as the hammer.

Mania – Psychotic affective reaction involving speeding up of thought processes and motor behavior and exaggerated feelings of optimism.

Mean – A measurement of central tendency that is computed by dividing the sum of a set of scores by the number of scores in the set, otherwise known as the arithmetic mean or average.

Median – A measure of central tendency; the middle score of a distribution, or the one that divides a distribution in half.

Medical model – A model of psychopathology in which pathological behaviors are viewed as symptoms of a disease.

Medulla (medulla oblongata) – The lowest and most posterior part of the brain, which is connected to the spinal cord. It contains several kinds of nuclei, especially those concerned with breathing, heartbeat, and blood pressure.

Mental retardation – A designation for exceptional subjects whose IQ scores are below the -2 standard deviations from the mean of a normal probability distribution of intelligence test scores, generally a score below 68.

Mental set – The tendency to respond in a given way regardless of the requirements of the situation. Sets sometimes facilitate performance and sometimes impair it. (Impairment is referred to as "functional fixedness.")

Minnesota Multiphasic Personality Inventory (MMPI) – A widely used empirically derived paper-and-pencil personality test designed to provide a measure of a subject's similarity to various psychopathological groups.

Mode – The score value that occurs most frequently in a given set of scores.

Modeling – In social learning theory, a form of learning in which the subject imitates the actions or reactions of another person. In behavior modification therapy, a technique based on imitation and perceptual learning.

Moro reflex – An automatic response shown by most normal infants to a startling stimulus, it involves throwing the arms to the side, extending the fingers, and then curving the hands back to the midline.

Morpheme – The smallest part of a word that conveys meaning and cannot be further subdivided without destroying the meaning; the units into which phonemes are arranged to make a language.

Myelin sheath – The fatty, or lipid, substance that surrounds the axons of some neurons. The greater the degree of myelinization, the greater the speed of transmission of neural impulses. The sheath is whitish in color.

Narcissistic – Self-centered, egotistical gratification-oriented; characteristic of the infant and of persons whose personalities retain infantile features.

Negative reinforcement – In operant conditioning, where reinforcement is paired with or contingent upon the termination of an aversive stimulus. Thus the absence of the stimulus condition strengthens or maintains a response.

Neocortex – The outer, highly developed, convoluted covering of the brain. It is the most recently evolved neural tissue.

Nerve – A bundle of axons from many neurons. Outside of the central nervous system, it runs from one point in the body to another and carries nerve impulses; used synonymously with neuron.

Nerve impulse – A change in polarity in the membrane of a nerve fiber that is propagated along the length of the fiber when its initial segment is stimulated above threshold; an action potential.

Nervous system – The brain and spinal cord, plus all of the neurons traveling throughout the rest of the body. It is a communication system, carrying information throughout the body.

Neuron – The basic structural unit of the nervous system, composed of a cell body, an axon, and one or more dendrites; its function is to send and receive messages.

Neurosis – Any of several less severe personality disturbances instigated and maintained for the purpose of contending with stress and avoiding anxiety, characterized by anxiety and rigid and unsuccessful attempts to reduce it.

Norepinephrine – An excitatory neurotransmitter substance found in the brain and in the sympathetic division of the autonomic nervous system.

Norm – A representative standard for performance or behavior; an established rule for identifying desirable behavior.

Normal curve – A mathematically defined curve that is bell-shaped and in which the mean, median, and mode are all in the same interval; it is the graphic representation of the normal probability distribution.

Null hypothesis – States that the independent variable will have no effect on the dependent variable.

Object permanence – A term in Piaget's theory of development which refers to a child's belief that an object continues to exist even though it is no longer visible.

Obsession – An idea, often irrational or unwanted, usually associated with anxiety, that persists or frequently recurs and cannot be dismissed by the individual.

Operant conditioning – A type of learning involving an increase in the probability of a response occurring as a result of reinforcement. Much of the experimental work of B. F. Skinner investigates the principles of operant conditioning (see Classical conditioning). Also referred to as instrumental conditioning.

Optic chiasm – A structure on the base of the brain that transmits the impulses from the receptors in the eye to the brain. In man, half of the optic fibers cross to the opposite hemisphere at the optic chiasm thus

providing information from both eyes to each hemisphere.

Organ of Corti – The lining on the basilar membrane of the inner ear that contains the hair cells which are the receptors for hearing.

Organic disorder – An emotional problem resulting from biological causes, usually from impairment of brain functioning.

Ossicles – Three tiny bones in the middle ear which transmit the sound vibrations from the eardrum to the cochlea.

Palmar reflex – The grasping reflex that a newborn infant exhibits when an object is placed in his or her hand.

Parasympathetic nervous system – A division of the autonomic nervous system which functions to maintain and conserve bodily resources.

Partial reinforcement effect – The finding that responses conditioned under partial reinforcement are more resistant to extinction than are those conditioned under continuous reinforcement.

Percentile – The score value below which a certain percent of cases falls. Thus, the 50th percentile on an examination is the raw score below which 50 percent of examinees fall.

Perception – The reception of information through sensory receptors and interpretation of that information so as to construct meaningfulness about one's world.

Perceptual defense – Failure to recognize stimuli that are threatening because of their relation to unconscious conflicts.

Peripheral nervous system (PNS) – Those nerves outside the central nervous system; it has two subdivisions, the somatic and autonomic systems. It contains all the neurons connecting to muscles, glands, and sensory receptors.

Phobia – An intense, compelling, and irrational fear of something; according to analytic theory it involves displacement of anxiety onto a situation that is not dangerous or only mildly dangerous.

Phoneme – The smallest unit of sound that has meaning in the language, generally consisting of a single sound such as a vowel.

Pituitary – An endocrine gland located at the base of the brain consisting of an anterior portion that controls other glands and growth and a posterior portion that is involved in metabolism. Because it regulates other glands it is sometimes referred to as the "master gland."

Placebo – A chemically inert material that has the same appearance as an active drug; allows psychologists to test the effects of the expectations of subjects who believe they are actually taking a drug; by analogy, the "placebo effect" is any situation in which subjects believe they are experiencing a manipulation by the experimenter when in fact they are not.

Polygraph – An instrument used to record various physiological measures such as galvanic skin response, heart rate, and so on. The lie detector is a common form of a polygraph.

Positive reinforcement – A type of event in which the presence of a stimulus condition strengthens or maintains a response.

Postsynaptic neuron – A neuron that receives the information (transmitter substance) from the axon of a presynaptic neuron.

Preconceptual thought – The first substage of the period of preoperational thought, beginning around age 2 and lasting until 4. It is so called because a child has not yet developed the ability to classify and therefore has an incomplete understanding of concepts.

Predictive validity – The degree to which a test measures what it is supposed to measure.

Prejudice – Attitude held toward members of another group that is emotionally, rigidly, or inflexibly felt and acted on, and negative.

Presynaptic neuron – The neuron whose axon releases transmitter substance into the synaptic cleft thereby transmitting information across the synapse to the postsynaptic neuron.

Primacy effect – In verbal learning, the tendency to recall items at the beginning of the list better than items in the middle. There is little proactive interference at this point.

Proactive interference – In learning, the negative influence of previously learned material on the recall of new material. When the influence is on the learning of the new material, it is called negative transfer.

Projection – A Freudian defense mechanism whereby the individual protects his ego from the recognition of an undesirable id impulse by relocating the impulse in another person.

Projective test – A relatively unstructured test designed so as to enhance the likelihood that the test-taker's motives and conflicts, and his style of dealing with them, will be revealed in his responses.

Proprioceptors – Receptors that sense position and movement of the limbs and the body in space. The principal proprioceptors are Pacinian corpuscles, muscle spindles, Golgi tendon organs, semicircular canals, utricles, and saccules.

Psychiatrist – A physician (M.D.) with specialized training in the treatment of mental illness.

Psychosis – A severe psychological disorder characterized by gross distortion of reality or by loss of reality testing, inability to distinguish between reality and fantasy, hallucinations, and/or delusions.

Punishment – The presentation of an unpleasant stimulus or removal of a pleasant stimulus for the purpose of eliminating undesirable behavior.

Random sample – A sample of cases drawn from some larger population in such a way that every member of the population has an equal chance of being drawn for the sample.

Rapid eye movement (REM) – One component of paradoxical sleep, characterized by rapid eye movements, an EEG like that of light sleep, and difficulty in waking. Dreams are thought to occur in this stage of sleep.

Ratio schedules – Partial reinforcement schedules in which the reinforcement delivered is based upon the number of correct responses made.

Reaction formation – A Freudian defense mechanism whereby the individual behaves in a manner opposite to his or her inclinations. Reaction formation is illustrated by an individual who intensely desires someone but is unable to obtain that person and, consequently, shows evidence of disliking that person. Results from unconscious or repressed desires or traits.

Reflex – An automatic response to a stimulus dependent on unlearned neural connections; exhibiting reflexive behavior.

Refractory period (phase) – Time interval, usually following a response, during which almost no stimulus will produce another response.

Regression – A defense mechanism of neurotic behavior, symbolic of returning to earlier period of development.

Regression to the mean – The tendency for extreme measures on some variable to be closer to the group mean when remeasured, due to unreliability of measurement.

Reinforcement – A stimulus occurring after a response that increases the probability of the response.

Reliability – The degree to which a test score remains stable over repeated measurements.

Retinal disparity – The slight difference in stimulus patterns produced on the two retinas of the eyes from one object; an important depth cue, also referred to as "binocular disparity."

Retroactive inhibition (interference) – Difficulty in recalling learned information because of something learned after the information one is trying to recall.

Retrograde amnesia – Forgetting of past events (i.e., before the amnesia) caused by physiological or psychological trauma.

Rods – The visual receptors which function primarily in dim or dark conditions; they are located toward the periphery of the eye and operate only in a black-and-white dimension.

Sample – A set of elements drawn from a population; an attempt should be made to make the sample as representative as possible of the population when the sample is to be used as the database for research.

Schedules of reinforcement – Ways of arranging partial reinforcement according to either a time interval or the number of responses made by the subject.

Secondary reinforcers – Originally neutral stimuli that come to function as reinforcers as the result of their learned association with primary reinforcers or through exchange for a reward, as in token economy therapy.

Self-actualization (Maslow) – The process or act of developing one's potentiality, achieving an awareness of one's identity and fulfilling oneself; the highest level of need.

Semantic memory – Retention of rules, knowledge of our language, and other material not specifically related to particular places, times, or events.

Semantics – The study of the relation of words, signs, and symbols to what they mean or denote.

Sensation – The simplest form of experience resulting from stimulation of a sense organ; a feeling.

Shaping – In operant conditioning, the procedure whereby the desired behavior is gradually "put together" by reinforcing the series of successive steps which culminate in the final response.

Social comparison – The process of determining one's own standards or standing on the basis of the behavior of others or using the behavior of others for purposes of evaluating one's own behavior, particularly in situations of uncertainty.

Social facilitation – Phenomenon in which the mere presence of other persons, as an audience or as co-workers, without any verbal exchange, increases individual performance.

Spontaneous recovery – In classical conditioning, the reoccurrence of an extinguished response following a rest period between extinction and retesting, and with no retraining.

Standard deviation – A measure of the variability or spread of scores in a group. The standard deviation is the square root of the average of the squared deviations from the arithmetic mean of the group.

Standardization – The establishment of norms or standards for administering, scoring, and interpreting a psychological test. It usually involves administering the test to a large group of people representative of those for whom the test is intended.

Sublimation – A defense mechanism in which an acceptable activity is substituted for an unacceptable activity or motive.

Superego – In Freudian theory, the part of the personality developing out of the ego during childhood. It contains values, morals, and basic attitudes as learned from parents and society.

Synapse – The space between the terminal button of an axon and the membrane or dendrites of another neuron. Transmitter substance flows across this space completing the circuit.

Systematic desensitization – Type of behavior therapy developed by Wolpe to help people overcome fears and anxiety. It involves step-by-step classical conditioning in which an anxiety-producing stimulus (CS) is paired with relaxation (CR).

Tabula rasa – In reference to the mental content of a newborn, the empiricist notion that the mind is initially a "blank tablet" to be inscribed upon by experience.

Test-retest reliability – Reliability estimated by giving the same test on two occasions and finding the correlation between the scores for the two administrations. Since the test is unchanged, differences from test to retest reflect either change or inconsistency of the individual from one occasion to another.

Trait – In respect to personality, a relatively persistent and consistent characteristic or attribute that serves to distinguish one person from another.

Transference (psychoanalytic theory) – The stage of therapy in which the patient begins to respond to the analyst as though the analyst were some significant person (e.g., mother or father) in the patient's past.

Unconditioned response (UCR) – In classical conditioning, the response elicited automatically, without any training, by the presentation of the unconditioned stimulus (UCS).

Unconditioned stimulus (UCS) – In classical conditioning, a stimulus that can elicit a response in the absence of conditioned learning.

Validity – The degree to which a test measures what it is supposed to measure as determined by a criterion.

Whorfian hypothesis – The assumption that the form of expression in a language directs the form of thought processes that develop.

Yerkes-Dodson law – A statement that performance is a curvilinear function of arousal or motivation, showing first an increase and then a decrease as arousal or motivation is increased.

Young-Helmholtz theory – Theory of color vision, holding that there are three kinds of color receptors (cones), each for a different primary color, and that any color experience involves a combination of stimulation of the three types of receptors.

Index

Superego, 70
Surveys, 16
Sympathetic nervous system, 25
Synapses, 23
Synaptic gap, 23
Syntax, 50
Systematic desensitization, 85–86

T

Telegraphic speech, 50
Temporal lobes, 26
Testing. *See also* CLEP *entries*
    reliability and, 95–96
    standardization and, 52, 96
Testosterone, 91–92
Test-retest reliability, 95
Test-taking tips, 9
Texture gradients, 31
Thalamus, 25
Theoretical orientations, 13–14
Thinking, 49–50
    Piaget's stages of cognitive
    development and, 62–64
Threshold
    absolute, 29
    difference, 29–30
Titchener, Edward, 13
Token economies, 86
Top-down information
    processing, 32

Traits, 73
Transference, 84
True self, 72
Trust vs. mistrust, 65
Two-factor theory of emotion, 58
Two-word stage, 50

U

Unconditional positive regard, 72
Unconditioned response (UR), 42
Unconditioned stimulus (US), 42
Undifferentiated schizophrenia, 79

V

Validity of tests, 96
Variable interval schedules, 44
Variable ratio schedules, 44
Ventromedial hypothalamus
    (VH), 56
Vesicles, 23
Vicarious learning, 45

W

Waxy flexibility, 79
Weapons effect, 92
Weber's Law, 29
Weight, set point for, 56
Wernicke's area, 26
Working memory, 51
Wundt, Wilhelm, 13